1981

D1058935

A Concept of Corporate Planning

A Concept of
Corporate Planning

by
RUSSELL L. ACKOFF
University of Pennsylvania

WILEY-INTERSCIENCE, A DIVISION OF JOHN WILEY & SONS
New York • Chichester • Brisbane • Toronto

Library of Congress Catalogue Card Number: 74–100318

ISBN 0 471 00290 9

Printed in the United States of America

10

To
NEIL JESSOP
whose death would have been untimely
whenever it had occurred

PREFACE

There is no lack of literature on the subject of corporate planning, nor is there a lack of opportunity for managers to hear lectures on the subject. In fact it has become difficult to avoid either. However, I have the impression, derived from discussion of the subject with many managers separately and collectively, that most of them do not have a clear idea of what planning is or, more important, what it should be. There is also confusion over what a plan should contain, how planning should be conducted and organized, and what values can be derived from it. Perhaps the persistence of these questions, despite the multiplication of efforts to answer them, is due to the fact that most of the literature and lectures on the subject tend to be filled with either platitudes or technicalities. Platitudes are easy to understand but are not useful. The technicalities tend to be more useful but less understandable.

I have tried to address myself to those questions about planning in which most managers seem to be interested and to do so in a way that provides answers that are both understandable and useful. Where I have not been able to do so I have tried to indicate where the difficulty lies. Mostly I have tried to develop a concept of planning in the round, to deal with the whole subject. What I have produced may well be more a philosophy of planning than a guide to it. I have certainly not produced a handbook, a *how to do it* book. This is more a *what should be done*, a *who should do it*, and a *why* book. It is much more concerned with the objectives and logic of the planning process than with specific techniques and tools that can be used in this process. Perhaps this is what a Manager's Guide to Corporate Planning should be.

Because of the limits of my experience the concept of planning developed here is primarily applicable to "homogeneous" corporations; that is, to ones with interrelated sets of activities. This does not exclude companies that have diversified outputs if their diversification has a logic dictated either by the nature of the inputs (the materials or services that it consumes), or the processes by which it transforms inputs into outputs, or the consumers of these outputs. The most apparent exceptions to these conditions are conglomerates and holding companies. I have not been involved in planning with such organizations. I believe, but do not know, that much of the concept developed here is applicable to them. However, I do know that the concept is applicable to their parts.

On the other hand, the concept of planning developed here has been applied to corporations of every size, from the very large to the very small. Therefore size of organization is not relevant to consideration of the applicability of the ideas put forward in the book. In fact these ideas, with only minor modification, have been employed in national, and other types of public, planning. To those involved in public planning it will be apparent that much, if not most, of what is written here is relevant in such planning.

In a sense the underlying theme of this book is the value of a marriage of management and management science in planning. By "management science" I mean the application of scientific methods—that is, the logic of scientific inquiry, not necessarily the techniques and tools that it has yielded—to the problems of management. Thus a management scientist can come from any of a large number of disciplines. What makes him a management scientist is not what he knows about management, but what he knows about using the methods of science in solving management problems.

Among the management sciences, operations research has a special role. It is an interdisciplinary activity that is concerned with the design and management of large, complex, organized man-machine systems. (See Ackoff and Rivett, 1963, for a detailed discussion of this field.) Most of the specific procedures, techniques, and tools discussed in this book have been developed in the practice of operations research.

In my concept of the management sciences and operations research the behavioral sciences play a major role. Without the participation of behavioral scientists many of the procedures discussed cannot be carried out effectively. I do not single out their contribution, nor that of representatives of any other discipline, because I assume that the research discussed is always interdisciplinary. In my opinion such research should involve representation of the formal sciences (logic, mathematics, and statistics), the physical sciences or fields of engineering based on them, and the behavioral sciences.

In preparing this work I have accumulated debts to many. The largest of these is to Eric Trist, who suggested many improvements in the manuscript and provided a great deal of encouragement. I am also indebted to Frank Calcerano of Western Electric, David B. Hertz of McKinsey and Company, Harper Moulton of IBM, Hoke Simpson of Columbia University, and E. Leonard Arnoff of The Institute of Management Sciences, who have allowed me to speak about planning to managers and management scientists so often that I have begun to believe I might have something to say on the subject.

I am particularly indebted to Jeanne Gibstein, my gal Monday-through-Friday, who has helped in preparing the manuscript for publication.

RUSSELL L. ACKOFF

Philadelphia
September 1969

CONTENTS

A Concept of Corporate Planning

Chapter 1

THE NATURE AND CONTENT
OF PLANNING

INTRODUCTION

Wisdom is the ability to see the long-run consequences of current actions, the willingness to sacrifice short-run gains for larger long-run benefits, and the ability to control what is controllable and not to fret over what is not. Therefore the essence of wisdom is concern with the future. It is not the type of concern with the future that the fortune teller has; he only tries to predict it. The wise man tries to *control* it.

Planning is the design of a desired future and of effective ways of bringing it about. It is an instrument that is used by the wise, but not by the wise alone. When conducted by lesser men it often becomes an irrelevant ritual that produces short-run peace of mind, but not the future that is longed for.

Recently I asked three corporate executives what decisions they had made in the last year that they would not have made were it not for their corporate plans. All had difficulty in identifying one such decision. Since each of their plans were marked "secret" or "confidential," I also asked them how their competitors might benefit from the possession of their plans. Each answered with embarrassment that their competitors would not benefit. Yet these executives were strong advocates of corporate planning.

The need for corporate planning is so obvious and so great that it is hard for anyone to be against it. But it is even harder to make such planning useful. Planning is one of the most complex and difficult intellectual activities in which man can engage. Not to do it well is not a sin, but to settle for doing it less than well is.

We do not yet understand corporate planning well enough to prepare a handbook on it. At present, and for some time to come,

1

planning will have to be tailored to the unique characteristics of the organization and situation in which it is carried out. Nevertheless some guidance at a fairly general level is possible. We can strive for an appreciation of what planning can do, a philosophy with which it can be approached, a concept of how it can be organized and systematized, and an awareness of the best methods, techniques, and tools that can be incorporated into it.

The science relevant to planning has developed rapidly in the recent past. However, even the best planning of which we are capable requires at least as much art as it does science. I am as interested in improving the art as I am in improving the science. Nowhere is the successful blending of the two more critical than it is here.

The principal contribution of scientists to planning may not lie in the development and use of relevant techniques and tools but rather in their systematization and organization of the planning process, and in the increased awareness and evaluation of this process that their presence produces.

THE NATURE OF PLANNING

Planning is clearly a decision-making process; but equally clearly not all decision making is planning. Not so clear, however, are the characteristics that make it a special kind of decision making. It is special in three ways.

1. Planning is something we do in advance of taking action; that is, it is *anticipatory decision-making*. It is a process of deciding what to do and how to do it before action is required. If we desire a certain state of affairs at some future time and it takes time to decide what to do and how to do it, we must make the necessary decisions before taking action. If these decisions could be taken quickly without loss of efficiency, planning would not be required.

2. Planning is required when the future state that we desire involves a set of interdependent decisions; that is, a *system of decisions*. A set of decisions forms a system if the effect of each decision in the set on the relevant outcome depends on at least one other decision in the set. Some of the decisions in the set may

be complex, others simple. But the principal complexity in planning derives from the interrelatedness of the decisions rather than from the decisions themselves; for example, in planning a house, a decision to place the living room in a particular corner has an effect on the location of every other room and hence on the "performance" of the house as a whole.

Sets of decisions that require planning have the following important characteristics:

a. They are too large to handle all at once. Therefore planning must be divided into stages or phases that are performed either sequentially by one decision-making body, or simultaneously by different bodies, or by some combination of sequential and simultaneous efforts. Planning must be staged or, put another way, it must itself be planned.

b. The set of necessary decisions cannot be subdivided into independent subsets. Hence a planning problem cannot be broken down into independent subplanning problems. The subplanning problems must be interrelated. This means that decisions made early in the planning process must be taken into account when making decisions later on in the process and *the earlier decisions must be reviewed in light of the decisions made subsequent to them.* This is why planning must be carried out before action is required.

These two systemic properties of planning make clear why planning is not an act but a *process,* a process that has no natural conclusion or end point. It is a process that (it is to be hoped) approaches a "solution," but it never quite gets there, for two reasons. First, there is no limit to the amount of reviewing of previous decisions that is possible. The fact that action is eventually required, however, makes it necessary to settle for what one has at some point in time. Second, both the system being planned for and its environment change during the planning process, and it is therefore never quite possible to take all such changes into account. The need to continuously update and "maintain" a plan derives in part from this fact.

3. Planning is a process that is directed toward producing one or more future states which are desired and which are not expected to occur unless something is done. Planning is thus concerned both with avoiding incorrect actions and with reducing

the frequency of failure to exploit opportunities. Obviously, if one believes that the natural course of events will bring about all that is desired, there is no need to plan. Thus planning always has both a pessimistic and an optimistic component. The pessimism lies in the belief that unless something is done a desired future state is not likely to occur. The optimism lies in the belief that something can be done to increase the chance that the desired state will occur.

Summarizing, we can say that planning is a process that involves making and evaluating each of a set of interrelated decisions before action is required, in a situation in which it is believed that unless action is taken a desired future state is not likely to occur, and that, if appropriate action is taken, the likelihood of a favorable outcome can be increased.

TACTICAL AND STRATEGIC PLANNING

The distinction between tactical and strategic planning is often made but is seldom made clear. Decisions that appear to be strategic to one person may appear to be tactical to another. This suggests that the distinction is relative rather than absolute. Indeed this is the case. Much of the confusion and apparent ambiguity derive from the fact that the difference between strategic and tactical planning is three dimensional.

1. The longer the effect of a plan and the more difficult it is to reverse, the more strategic it is. Therefore strategic planning is concerned with decisions that have enduring effects that are difficult to reverse; for example, next week's production planning is more tactical and less strategic than planning a new plant or distribution system. Strategic planning is long-range planning. Tactical planning is of shorter range. But "long" and "short" are relative terms and therefore so are "strategic" and "tactical." In general strategic planning is concerned with the longest period worth considering; tactical planning is concerned with the shortest period worth considering. Both types of planning are necessary. They complement each other. They are like the head and tail of a coin: we can look at them separately, even discuss them separately, but we cannot separate them in fact.

2. The more functions of an organization's activities are affected by a plan, the more strategic it is. That is, strategic planning is broad in scope. Tactical planning is narrower. "Broad" and "narrow" are also relative concepts thus adding to the relativity of "strategic" and "tactical." A strategic plan for a department may be a tactical plan from the point of view of a division. Other things being equal, planning at the corporate level is generally more strategic than planning at any organizational level below it.

3. Tactical planning is concerned with selecting means by which to pursue specified goals. The goals are normally supplied by a higher level in the organization. Strategic planning is concerned with both formulation of the goals and selection of the means by which they are to be attained. Thus strategic planning is oriented to ends as well as to means. However, "means" and "ends" are also relative concepts; for example, "advertising a product" is a means to the end of "selling it." "Selling it," however, is a means to the end of "profit," and profit is itself a means to many other ends.

Put briefly, strategic planning is long-range corporate planning that is ends oriented (but not exclusively so). It should be apparent that both strategic and tactical planning are required in order to maximize progress.

THE PARTS OF PLANNING

Planning should be a continuous process and hence no plan is ever final; it is always subject to revision. A plan therefore is not the final product of the planning process; it is an interim report. It is a record of a complex set of interacting decisions that may be partitioned in many different ways. Different planners prefer different ways of subdividing the decisions that must be made. As long as all the relevant decisions are taken into account, the various ways of dividing a plan into parts are largely a matter of personal preference or style. Hence we need not occupy ourselves with the relative advantages and disadvantages of different ways of partitioning a plan.

The order in which the parts of planning are given here does not represent the order in which they should be completed. Recall that the set of decisions involved in planning cannot be subdivided into independent subsets. Hence the parts of a plan and the phases of a planning process that produce them must interact. The order in which I present the parts therefore reflects only my opinion of the order in which it is usually most convenient to *start* thinking about them.

The parts are only briefly identified at this point since each one is subsequently discussed in a chapter of its own.

1. *Ends*: specification of objectives and goals.

2. *Means*: selection of policies, programs, procedures, and practices by which objectives and goals are to be pursued.

3. *Resources*: determination of the types and amounts of resources required, how they are to be generated or acquired, and how they are to be allocated to activities.

4. *Implementation*: design of decision-making procedures and a way of organizing them so that the plan can be carried out.

5. *Control*: design of a procedure for anticipating or detecting errors in, or failures of, the plan and for preventing or correcting them on a continuing basis.

These are the parts that in my opinion a plan *should* contain. Many plans do not contain them. Which of these parts a plan does contain, and the relative amounts of attention they receive, is largely a matter of the philosophy that lies behind the planning.

PHILOSOPHIES OF PLANNING

As planners have become more self-conscious and aware of the process in which they are engaged, certain attitudes, concepts, philosophies, or what might even be called strategies of planning have become visible to students of the process. There appear to be three dominant philosophies. They are presented here in their "pure" form, although it will be apparent that most planning involves some mixture of them. Nevertheless most planning is dominated by one of the three points of view, which I call *satisficing, optimizing,* and *adaptivizing*. These names are not very good because their connotations are vague and ambiguous. Unfortunately I have not been able to find better ones. I certainly have no objection, therefore, to the substitution of any other names. The most prevalent—namely, satisficing—is discussed first, and the least prevalent—adaptivizing—last.

Satisficing

"Satisficing" is a remarkably useful term that was coined by Herbert A. Simon to designate efforts to attain some level of satisfaction, but not necessarily to exceed it. To satisfice is to do "well enough," but not necessarily "as well as possible." The level of attainment that defines "satisfaction" is one that the decision maker is willing to settle for.

Satisficing planning begins with setting objectives and goals that are believed to be both feasible and desirable. Attribution of these properties to objectives and goals is usually based on consensus among the planners.

Objectives and goals are usually formulated by satisficers either in terms of commonly used measures of performance (e.g., profit or return on investment), or in qualitative terms (e.g., good employee relations). In the extreme the satisficer seems to operate on the principle that, if one cannot measure what one wants, one should want either what he can measure or does not want to measure. For example, for most managers the objective of advertising is to increase sales. However, the increase of sales produced by advertising is difficult (but not impossible) to measure. Recall of messages, the number of "impressions" that they make, or changes in "attitudes" produced by them are apparently easier to measure. Therefore the satisficing marketing planner tends to state advertising objectives in terms of recall, impressions, and attitudes, rather than in terms of increased sales.

It is quite common for the satisficing planner to set only a few simple goals; for example, to increase earning annually by 10 percent, or market share annually by 5 percent. He normally does not concern himself about providing a way of mediating conflicts that might arise between such goals; for example, if a specified market share and amount of profit cannot be simultaneously obtained in the short run, the satisficer is not likely to provide management with a basis for determining the tradeoffs between the two.

The satisficer normally sets objectives and goals first. Since he does not seek to set these as "high" as possible, only "high enough," he has to revise them only if they do not turn out to be feasible. Once the objectives and goals are set, he seeks only one feasible and acceptable way of obtaining them; again not necessarily the best possible way.

The satisficer's orientation is much like the political notion of the "art of the possible." In what is seldom a systematic procedure he tries to "maximize" feasibility, which he seldom explicitly defines. He tries to do so by (a) minimizing the number and magnitude of departures from current policies and practices, (b) at most specifying modest increases in resource requirements, and (c) making no large changes in organizational structure (since these usually meet with opposition from those affected).

In their efforts to obtain a feasible set of procedures, programs, and policies satisficers seldom systematically formulate and evaluate many alternatives because any feasible set will satisfy them. They are usually more concerned with identifying past deficiencies produced by current policies than with exploiting future opportunities. Therefore, in a sense, the satisficing planner tends to enter the future facing the past.

In resource planning most satisficers are preoccupied with one resource, money. Their orientation is dominated by emphasis on the financial aspects of the business. They seldom give detailed consideration to manpower, facilities and equipment, and materials and services. They do not do so because they believe that, if sufficient funds are available, any other type of resource that is required can be acquired when needed. This can lead to difficulty when significant lead times are needed to acquire or produce required resources; for example, manpower trained in the company or plants that require several years to build.

Satisficing planners reflect a prevalent proccupation of executives with finance. Such planners emphasize projections or extrapolations of current financial trends and budgeting. Financial forecasting and budgeting are essential parts of planning, but they tend to dominate the satisficers' thinking and to minimize or exclude other essential parts of the planning process.

Satisficers tend to shy away from organizational changes because they often spawn controversy. Their plans seldom require reorganization of the corporation being planned for. They prefer not to "rock the boat."

Planners oriented to satisficing normally deal with only one forecast of the future, and deal with this as though it were virtually certain to come about. Hence they produce what might be called point plans. They seldom deal explicitly with the possibilities, let alone the probabilities. They assume that, if the unexpected should occur, the organization is capable of coping with it. Hence they seldom design formalized systems for controlling a plan after its implementation.

The satisficing approach to planning is usually defended with the hard-to-refute argument that it is better to produce a feasible plan that is not optimal than an optimal plan that is not feasible. But this argument is based on the belief that consideration of feasibility cannot be incorporated into consideration of optimality. This is not true. It is possible to seek the *best feasible plan.* Optimality can (and should) be defined so as to take feasibility into account, although even optimizers seldom try to do so. Such an effort has the advantage of forcing the planner to examine critically criteria of feasibility—criteria that are seldom made explicit in the satisficing process. Furthermore the truism, "a feasible plan that is not optimal is better than one that is optimal but infeasible," should be balanced by another equally potent truism, "the approximate attainment of an optimal plan may be better than the exact attainment of one that is merely satisfactory."

Not surprisingly, satisficing planning seldom produces a radical departure from the past. It usually yields conservative plans that comfortably continue most current policies, correcting only obvious deficiencies. Such planning therefore appeals to organizations that are more concerned with survival than with development and growth.

The most serious deficiency of this type of planning is that it seldom increases understanding of either the system being planned for or the planning process itself. The satisficer tends to use only available knowledge and understanding of the system; he seldom engages in research designed to expand such knowledge and understanding. His planning is not research oriented. For this and other reasons his planning usually requires less time, money, and technical skill than the other types of planning. This of course is one of its principal attractions.

Optimizing

In this second type of planning an effort is made not just to do well enough, but to do as well as possible. The optimizing approach to planning has been made possible largely by the development and use of mathematical models of the systems being planned for. For those who are not familiar with such models a brief discussion of their origin, nature, and use may be helpful.

Models and Optimization. Experimentation is an essential part of science. But large systems (whether solar, corporate, or governmental) cannot be brought into a laboratory nor can experiments be conducted on them as a whole in their natural environment. Therefore, since experimentation is necessary to gain understanding and control over such systems and experiments cannot be conducted on them, experiments must be conducted on something other than the system under study. Clearly, if such experimentation is to yield knowledge relevant to the system, it must be conducted on something that is *like* the system under study. *Models* are representations of systems that serve this purpose. They may be physical representations (such as model airplanes in wind tunnels or model ships in tow tanks), graphic representations (such as diagrams and graphs), or symbolic representations (such as mathematical equations).

An experiment conducted on a model of a system is called a *simulation.* When symbolic models are used, however, it is sometimes possible to determine what the results of an experiment would be without actually conducting it, by deductive processes (i.e., mathematical analysis). This can frequently save much time and effort, and yield more precise results than can be obtained by simulation.

The use of symbolic models is central in the methodology of operations research. These models vary widely in size, shape, and complexity; but, since they all deal with the process of decision making, they all have the same underlying structure. A decision model usually has two parts: an *objective function* and a set of one or more *constraints.*

An objective function is an equation of the following form:

performance of the system $(P) =$ some
relationship between (f) [controlled
variables (C) and uncontrolled variables (U)]

or, more simply,

$$P = f(C, U).$$

The measure of system performance is one that the system manager wishes to maximize or minimize (i.e., optimize). When multiple objectives are involved, a single measure of performance may nevertheless be possible. Decision and value theory are bodies of knowledge that are used in the construction of appropriate measures of performance. Such construction may be the most difficult part of the research process. But without an explicit criterion for evaluating alternative policies or practices how can one know how well he is performing, let alone assure himself that he is performing as well as possible?

The controlled variables are ones that the decision maker can manipulate; for example, the amount of money invested in various corporate activities, prices of products, and size and location of plants. The uncontrolled variables are ones that are not subject to the decision maker's control but which nevertheless affect performance of the system; for example, weather, general economic conditions, the behavior of competitors, technological developments, and the preferences of consumers.

The second part of a decision model usually consists of one or more symbolic statements in which the limits of the decision maker's control are precisely expressed; for example, if in a budgeting problem a corporation has to allocate funds to five divisions or departments, then the sum of these allocations must be equal to, or greater than, zero and it cannot exceed the total amount of money available to the company.

Such models represent both the decision and the system affected by it. It relates the performance of the system to what the decision maker can do about it.

Once a decision model has been constructed the researcher's problem is to find the values of the controlled variables which, subject to the constraints and under the specified uncontrolled conditions, optimize the system's performance. These optimizing values of the controlled variables are sought either by simulation or deductive analysis. In both these processes computers have come to play an increasingly important role. They enable the researcher to deal with models of a complexity that he could not feasibly deal with "by hand."

A very simple example of model construction is given in the Appendix, which also contains a nontechnical description of a model that was developed to optimize investment in research and development.

Back to Optimizing. As noted above, the optimizer tries to formulate corporate goals in quantitative terms and to combine them into a single measure of overall corporate performance. He may not succeed completely, but he usually manages to translate some vaguely formulated qualitative objectives into more precise quantitative terms. Furthermore he can sometimes transform a variety of goals into measures on a single scale (usually monetary) and hence can combine them into one general measure of performance. Unfortunately the optimizer tends to ignore goals that he cannot quantify. This can distort the value of his work and produce justifiable discomfort in the consuming managers who must moderate quantitative results with their own qualitative judgments on important problems that have not been taken into account.

The optimizing planner seeks the best available policies, programs, procedures, and practices by use of mathematical models. The success that such a planner has depends on how completely and accurately his models represent the system and on how well he can extract solutions from the model once it has been constructed. His capabilities are currently limited because he cannot construct one model that represents all aspects of a total corporate system. He must model it in parts and, because of the as yet unpenetrated complexity of some of the parts, he cannot model all of these. Therefore he tends to plan only for those units or aspects of a system for which he can construct and solve models. Sometimes his commitment to the approach that he calls "rational" justifies Ambrose Bierce's definition of this term: "Devoid of all delusions save those of observation, experience and reflection" (*The Devil's Dictionary*, 1911).

Efforts, even unsuccessful efforts, to develop truly optimal plans almost always produce a valuable by-product: a deeper understanding of the system being planned for. Unfortunately this understanding is not always communicated successfully to the managers involved.

The optimizer tries either (*a*) to minimize the resources required to obtain a specified level of performance, (*b*) to maximize the performance that can be attained with resources that are (or are expected to be) available, or (c) to obtain the best balance of costs (resources consumed) and benefits (performance). Explicit consideration of all types of resources is more common among optimizers than it is among satisficers, although optimizers also tend to emphasize financial resources. Operations researchers have developed models (and ways of solving them) that can and have been used to optimize the size and location of facilities, distribution of materials and goods to and among them and from them to customers, equipment replacement and maintenance policies, make-or-buy decisions, and many other decisions that are relevant to resource planning. They can do this even when future demand is uncertain; that is, when it can only be forecast in a way that is subject to error.

Planning for facilities, equipment, materials, and services is more likely to be treated adequately by optimizers than is personnel. Quantitative techniques for handling the latter are relatively undeveloped as yet, but they are being improved.

Optimizing planners seldom explicitly treat organizational structure because models of this aspect of a firm have only begun to be developed. By "organizational structure" I mean the way that the work done by an organization is divided into parts (e.g., by functions such as production and marketing, or by type of product, or by geographic region), and how work is assigned to parts of the organization. The structure is reflected not only in the responsibilities given to the parts of the organization but also in the measures of performance applied to them, because these define their objectives. The objective of organizational planning is to produce an organization that can effectively pursue its overall objectives and, specifically, carry out the plans that are produced.

At present the best that can be done is to optimize either complex structures relative to very simple problems or simple structures relative to complex problems. As yet we cannot optimize complex structures relative to complex problems. For example, we can determine how to divide responsibility for inventories between the purchasing and selling functions in such a relatively simple organization as a department store. But the optimal division of this responsibility for finished-goods inventory in a complex vertically integrated process (as in an oil company) is beyond our current capabilities.

Where quantitative optimization techniques alone are inadequate to produce the best organizational structure they can be combined with enlightened judgment to produce one that is approximately optimal. In general, attempts to optimize structure require extensive use of qualitative judgments. Too many optimizers prefer to avoid such judgments and hence either omit this important aspect of planning or turn it over to others whose output they do not integrate with their own.

Even the most detailed optimizing plan can be sabotaged by many small actions (or inactions) taken by individuals who separately or collectively are not motivated to act in a way that is compatible with planned objectives; for example, I have seen managers and other personnel who are in a unit that is planned to be dissolved over a specified period of time take actions that increase the difficulty of phasing out their operation. Implementation of a plan can never be mechanized. It always depends on the good will and cooperation of individuals and groups in the organization. Many optimizing planners tend to treat organizations and their parts as though they were completely programmable; they are not. Hence attention to the *motivation* of individuals and groups in the organization should be (but seldom is) an essential part of their planning. Where appropriate motivation does not exist it is the planner's responsibility to see to it that it is developed.

Finally optimizing planners can and do construct control systems that are capable of detecting and correcting for errors whose possibility has been anticipated; that is, they provide controls that determine when an organization has failed to meet its expectations, but do not determine when meeting its expectations constitutes a failure (i.e., when it has failed to exploit the unexpected). Opportunities that have not been anticipated generally knock only once. Not to answer the door is an error of *omission*. Incorrect action with respect to an anticipated opportunity is an error of *commission*. Optimizing controls are usually directed only against the latter.

Not everything that can happen can be anticipated. The number of unexpected things that do happen is too large to be handled by a centralized control unit such as are usually designed by optimizing planners. Every part of the organization should be made capable of exercising self-control and of responding effectively to the unexpected even when not controlled from above.

To summarize, the techniques of optimization have in general been more useful in tactical than in strategic planning. These techniques are currently applicable to only some aspects of strategic planning. They have considerable utility, but not if the cost of using them is omission of the aspects of planning to which they currently cannot be applied. An optimal comprehensive strategic plan is beyond our current capabilities, but planning that optimizes parts of the plan and integrates these with the other parts that have been treated by other than optimization techniques can be extremely useful. In other words, a planning procedure that employs quantitative optimization where possible and qualitative satisficing where necessary is likely to produce better results than either satisficing or optimizing alone can yield.

Adaptivizing

This type of planning is sometimes referred to as innovative planning. It is not prevalent today because we have neither developed a clear and comprehensive concept of it nor a systematized methodology for carrying it out. Therefore it is more an aspiration than a realization. However, adaptiveness can be designed into organizations to a greater extent than current practice would lead one to believe.

Adaptive planning has three main planks in its platform:

1. It is based on the belief that the principal value of planning does not lie in the plans that it produces but in the process of producing them. In effect the adaptivizing planner's slogan is, "Process is our most important product." Hence it holds that the value of planning to managers lies primarily in their participation in the process, not in their consumption of its product. From this it follows that effective planning cannot be done *to* or *for* an organization; it must be done *by* the responsible managers.

This point of view is well reflected in the following observation made by Eric Trist (1968, p. 26):

"Michel Crozier . . . who is carrying out a sociological study of the decision-making of the Ve Plan, has shown that the most important effect of French Planning lies not so much in the achieve-

ment of the targets as in the social learning released in the in-
numerable commissions which take part in making, carrying out,
and revising the plan."

2. Most of the current need for planning arises out of lack of
effective management and controls. Man produces most of the
messes that planning tries to eliminate or avoid. Therefore the
principal objective of planning should be to design an organization and a system for managing it that will minimize the future
need for *retrospective* planning—that is, planning directed toward
removing deficiencies produced by past decisions—and to do so
by reducing the possibility of such deficiencies being produced.
The objective is not to eliminate *prospective* planning: planning
that is directed toward creating a desired future.

3. Our knowledge of the future can be classified into three
types: certainty, uncertainty, and ignorance; each requires a different kind of planning: commitment, contingency, and responsiveness.

a. First, there are certain aspects of the future about which we
can be virtually certain. There are some future changes that may
be virtually inevitable and there are some "unchanges" that may
be also; that is, aspects of the environment that will remain stable.
To take some trivial examples, the percentage of males and females
in the population may not change, but the number of twenty-one-
years-olds in the United States may change from now to 1980.
However, this number can be estimated with virtual certainty.
The relatively certain aspects of the future may (and frequently
are) difficult to identify. A good deal of research may be required
to uncover them. They often become obvious only retrospectively;
for example, only now is it becoming obvious that there will be a
large demand for metering emissions of pollutants into air and
water.

With respect to those aspects of the future about which we can
be virtually certain, we can carry out *commitment* planning. But
even here the possibility of error should be taken into account by
providing appropriate controls. Continuous updating of estimates
of what is inevitable or unchanging is required. Furthermore
prudence dictates that commitments be made not any sooner than

necessary to accomplish the desired objective. It is not always best to be the first to try to exploit a perceived opportunity.

With tongue partly in cheek we can say that successful long-range planning involves, among other things, (1) uncovering the inevitable, (2) determining how to exploit it, and (3) taking credit for having brought it about. We return to this point in subsequent discussion.

b. Second, there are certain aspects of the future about which we cannot be relatively certain, but we can be reasonably sure of what the possibilities are; for example, we may not know what type of motor power will eventually replace the internal combustion engine in automobiles, but we can be reasonably sure that it will be either a "cleaned up" engine of the same type or one that is powered by steam or electrically, by a battery or fuel cell. In such cases *contingency* planning is required; that is, we should prepare a plan for each eventuality so that we can quickly exploit the opportunities that are presented when "the future makes up its mind."

Contingency planning is old hat in the military but is relatively rare in business; for example, in planning for a military invasion consideration is always given to each possible outcome of an operation and plans are made for each. Military planners do not wait to see what happens before planning what to do about it. They try to cover every possibility in advance, because time is "of the essence" once a possibility has become a reality.

c. Finally there are aspects of the future that we cannot anticipate; for example, natural or political catastrophes, or technological breakthroughs. We cannot prepare for these directly, but we can do so indirectly through *responsiveness* planning. Such planning is directed toward designing an organization and a system for managing it that can quickly detect deviations from the expected and respond to them effectively. Hence responsiveness planning consists of building responsiveness and flexibility into an organization.

The Nature of Adaptation. Adaptation is a response to a change (stimulus) that actually or potentially reduces the efficiency of a system's behavior, a response which prevents that reduction from occurring. The change may be either internal (within the system itself) or external (in its environment); for example, a change in managerial personnel that reduces corporate efficiency would be an internal stimulus, but a change in a competitor's pricing policy would be an external one.

Adaptive responses are also of two types. In the first, *passive* adaption, the system changes its behavior so as to perform more efficiently in a changing environment (e.g., a person putting on a sweater when he gets cold or a company reducing its costs and prices when the competition does). In the second, *active* adaptation, the system changes its environment so that its own present or future behavior is more efficient (e.g., turning up the heat when one gets cold in a house or bringing about legislation to prevent price cutting by competitors). (See F. E. Emery, 1967, for a more detailed discussion of this distinction.) These two types of adaptation can of course be combined.

Changes in the environment may be rapid and of short duration (e.g., changes in demand for a product from day to day), or slow and of long duration (e.g., introduction of a new product by a competitor). An adaptive organization should be capable of coping with both. Consider what is required to do so.

We obviously require flexibility of plant, equipment, and personnel. For example, the direction of traffic flow in the third Lincoln Tunnel connecting New Jersey and New York City can be reversed, depending on the change in demand from morning to evening. The same can be done to the two center lanes of an expressway in Chicago. Such flexibility can be planned for, frequently with considerable economies. Three tunnels, one of which is reversible, can carry the same load as four one-way tunnels because of the asymmetry of automobile traffic into and out of New York in the morning and evening. Ideally we would like to have facilities that can be used to serve any purpose and can expand and contract depending on demand. Such flexibility is possible only to a limited extent. Therefore demand itself must be at least partially controlled.

Control of demand in the short run and in the long run usually requires different approaches. Consider the long-run problem first.

A manufacturer of machine tools was subject to fluctuations in demand as great as two to one in successive years. This prevented effective use of facilities and personnel. The company looked for another highly cyclical, but countercyclical, product line that required the same technology as it was already using. It found such a class of products in highway-construction equipment and entered the business. By so doing it reduced variations in annual production loads to only a small fraction of what they had been previously.

Thus one way of obtaining control over the future is to reduce the variations one might expect in the behavior of essential parts of the system or its environment.

Consider another company that produces a raw material used in more than 3000 different forms. Of these about 10 percent accounted for all of the profits and most of the volume of business. Small orders for the remaining large number of small-volume unprofitable items led to frequent disruptions of production schedules, which were geared for long, continuous production runs of the high-volume profitable items. Marketing management refused to drop the small-volume unprofitable items from the company's product line or to raise their prices even to cover cost because—it argued—this would antagonize those customers who were also heavy consumers of the high-volume profitable items and would run the risk of losing them.

An optimizer's approach to this problem consisted of constructing a model of the production-inventory-sales system and deriving from it a way of scheduling the production line to meet the demand on it—a way that minimized the sum of the production, inventory, and shortage costs. The improvements yielded were significant but small.

An adaptivizer took a different approach. He found that by eliminating 4 percent of the least profitable items from the product line he could reduce production costs and increase profits by an amount equal to the improvement the optimizer had obtained. Therefore he concentrated on the marketing, not the production, system. He found that salesmen were given a base salary plus a percentage of the dollar value of their sales. This led him to design a new salesman incentive plan. It was profit (rather than volume) oriented; it paid no commission on sales of unprofitable items and higher commissions than before on profitable ones. The plan was so designed that, if salesmen continued to sell the same mix of items as they had before, their earnings would not change.

In the first year of this plan's operation sales of about half the unprofitable items in the product line virtually stopped, and sales of the profitable items increased significantly.

The optimizing planner generally takes the system structure for granted and seeks a course of action that best solves the problem. The adaptive planner, on the other hand, tries to change the system in such a way that more efficient behavior follows "naturally."

The principle of control used in the last example is one of the most important in adaptive planning because it provides an effective way of handling short- as well as long-range variations in the system. It involves motivating participants in the system to act in a way that is compatible with the interests of the organization as a whole, and it does this by providing incentives that make individual and organizational objectives more compatible.

Consider this principle in the realm of traffic control and how it might be used to induce people to use transportation facilities in such a way as to serve their own and their community's interests more effectively. First, the tolls for bridges, tunnels, and turnpikes, at least during periods of heavy demand, could be made inversely proportional to the number of passengers in a car. More specifically tolls would be based on the number of empty seats in an automobile. Thus a two-seat car with two passengers would have a lower toll than a six-seater with two, three, four, or five passengers. A six-seater with three passengers would have a lower toll than one with only two. This would encourage better occupancy of all cars and more use of smaller cars.

Second, tolls might be varied with demand. The heavier the demand for a facility, the higher the charges. Thus charges would be increased during peak hours and decreased during off hours. This would produce a more even use of facilities.

Adaptive thinking of course is not new. But planning that is primarily and systematically committed to producing more adaptive organizations is. We have only begun to exploit the possibilities of such planning. Those who do so most effectively are most likely to develop and exploit the potentialities of their organizations.

CONCLUSION

At the present time satisficing planning is the only one of the three approaches to which we can usually adhere completely. We cannot completely optimize and can only begin to adaptivize a plan. However, we can push our planning efforts to the frontiers of methodology and perhaps even advance those frontiers. The best we can do at present involves a mixture of approaches. This is not the only place that scientific methods and comon sense, and technology and judgment, are required to share the same bed.

The more that corporate planning is pushed from satisficing toward adaptivizing, the greater the requirement for scientific methods, techniques, and tools. The relevance of the management sciences and computer technology increases as we push out from the traditional concept of conventional planning. This does not mean that the need for management's expertise and participation decreases; to the contrary, it increases. Although it may be easier for managers who are planning on their own to satisfice, it is hardest for management scientists to carry out adaptive planning without the participation of managers.

Optimizing planning requires more understanding of an organization's behavior than does satisficing. Adaptive planning requires even more than does optimizing. Because adaptive planners operate largely through the manipulation of incentives and because they seek compatibility of collective, unit, and individual objectives, they must be aware of, and responsive to, values held by the organization as a whole, its parts, the individuals who make it up, and those organizations and individuals in its environment whose behavior affects the system planned for. Adaptive planning also requires understanding of the dynamics of values: the way values relate to needs and their satisfaction, how changes in needs produce changes in values, and what produces changes in needs. Thus the understanding of collective and individual behavior that is required by adaptive planning is considerably greater than that currently possessed by many corporate planners and managers.

Effective planning requires close collaboration of creative experts and managers in efforts to solve the many difficult problems involved. Such planning is costly and time consuming. But there is probably no other activity of a company that can yield so large a return on the investment; and there is probably no other activity that it can be so costly not to do.

Now we turn to detailed consideration of each of the five aspects of planning; first to the formulation of objectives and goals.

Chapter 2

OBJECTIVES AND GOALS

INTRODUCTION

Planning is predicated on the belief that the future can be improved by active intervention now. Therefore it presupposes some prediction of what is likely to come about if there is no planned intervention. Such a prediction can be called a *reference projection*. It attempts to specify what the future states of the organization being planned for will be if nothing new is done.

If the future that is described in the reference projection is satisfactory planning is not required. This implies that planners have a second type of projection, one that might be called *wishful*. This is a concept of where the organization wants to be and when it wants to be there. The difference between the reference and wishful projections defines the gap to be filled (it is to be hoped) by planning.

It would be very rare indeed for planners to expect to be able to fulfill all of an organization's aspirations; that is, to realize the wishful projection. Their task is to determine how closely they can approximate these aspirations. A description of how far they believe the organization can go toward fulfilling its aspirations can be called the *planned projection*. Therefore planning must begin with a reference projection and a wishful projection. It cannot terminate until it has produced a planning projection.

These projections involve describing possible states of the organization and determining the degrees to which they are desired. States or outcomes of behavior that are desired are *objectives*. An organization may desire either to *obtain* something that it does not currently have (e.g., a dominant share of its maket), or to *retain* something it already has (e.g., the dominant share in a particular area). Hence objectives may be either acquisitive or retentive.

Goals are objectives whose attainment is desired by a specified time within the period covered by the plan; for example, "to acquire our own distribution system by 1975" or "to increase our market share by 10 percent by 1975" are goals.

Objectives may be unattainable within the planning period, but they must be approachable within it; for example, "to turn out only products that are free of defects." Goals must be attainable within the planning period, but need not necessarily be attained. An objective which can never be attained but which can be approached without limit is called an *ideal*. (Vickers, 1965, discusses the difference between goals and objectives at length.)

The objective-and-goal formulation phase of planning should accomplish the following:

1. Specification of corporate objectives and their translation into goals. Such a translation constitutes a *schedule* for the attainment of goals.

2. Provision of an operational definition of each goal and specification of the measures to be used in evaluating progess with respect to each.

3. Elimination of (or provision of means for resolving) conflicts between goals; that is, for deciding what to do when progress toward one goal requires sacrificing progress toward another.

I shall consider each of these requirements in turn, but first an important characteristic of objectives should be examined in some detail.

STYLISTIC OBJECTIVES

Objectives, as I have noted, are *valued* states or outcomes. Some things are valued *instrumentally;* that is, because they can be used to acquire or retain something else of value. Money, for example, has an instrumental value—and so do tools, knowledge, and information. Other things are valued *intrinsically;* that is, for their own sake. I prefer black ink to green ink; I would use the latter only in desperation. But both types of ink are equally valuable to me instrumentally. The difference between them is intrinsic. It is a matter of *taste* or what the psychologists call a person's *style*. Style is to a large extent a matter of esthetics, and it is as important to organizations as it is to men and women.

Instrumentally valued states and outcomes—or *performance objectives*, as I call them—receive a good deal of attention in corporate planning; but intrinsic values or *stylistic objectives* seldom do. They should. For example, the managers of a hand-tool manufacturing company had asked for a plan to diversify and expand the growth possibilities of their company. When presented with diversification proposals, each of which involved extending the line of tools made, they rejected them one after another without what appeared to the planners to be adequate justification. Finally one of the planners in desperation made the offhand suggestion that the company manufacture electronic parts, and much to his surprise the managers expressed interest in that possibility. When pressed for an explanation, the managers revealed that they were bored with their current business and wanted to get some fun out of it. Therefore they wanted a "technological challenge." They eventually found it in valves and couplings, which presented such a challenge to them without departing too radically from their expertise.

Similarly a durable-goods company, which insisted that its only objective was to maintain a specified rate of increase in earnings per share, rejected a diversification plan that involved its going into packaged consumables. They did so on the grounds that dealing with such products was not their "style."

Formulating Stylistic Objectives: Scenarios

Every organization has very general stylistic, as well as performance, objectives that condition much of what it will and will not do. These objectives in effect define in qualitative terms the kind of activity in which the organization wants to be involved. It is important, therefore, to make these objectives explicit at an early stage of planning. This can be done if the planners address themselves to the question, What kind of business would the company most like to be in? Subsequent planning or time may change these aspirations, but an initial formulation of them provides a very good starting point for the planning process. An effective way of getting at these aspirations is through the use of *scenarios*.

Basically a scenario is a description of what the company might be at some specified time in the future. It is a qualitative and stylistic description, rather than one that is finance, and hence performance, oriented. It does not employ such usual ways of characterizing progress as profit, return on investment, earnings, debt, and so on; and it does not do so for a good reason.

Use of scenarios is based on the conviction that what a company becomes depends more on what it does than on what is done to it. Hence a company is taken as capable of fashioning almost any kind of future that it wants. Whether or not a particular direction of development turns out to be profitable depends primarily on the nature of the commitment that the company makes to creating that future. Thus scenarios are qualitative wishful projections of the company into the future.

There are of course an unlimited number of possible futures (and hence scenarios) that can be prepared for any particular company. However, it is usually sufficient for initial planning purposes to consider only a relatively few projections that define the major possibilities and feasibilities. These can be extracted from a flow diagram of the existing business, one that shows each major type of input (product or service) consumed by the business, and each major type of output produced by the company and consumed by others. The businesses suggested by these inputs and outputs are candidates for scenarios. In Figure 2.1 the flow diagram of a packaged food company is shown together with the scenario topics suggested by the diagram. Amplified, they are as follows:

1. The company could go into the agricultural business, initially to produce the raw materials from which its products are made.

2. It could go into the packaging business of which it is a very large consumer.

3. It could go into the plant-construction or equipment-manufacturing business. This possibility was not considered further because of the relatively small volume the company itself could guarantee and because the technology required is completely foreign to the company.

4. It could go into the business of supplying its wholesalers with trucks for lease, credit, warehouse space, and so on.

5. It could acquire wholesalers and thus go into that business itself.

6. It could produce some of the other products distributed by its wholesalers.

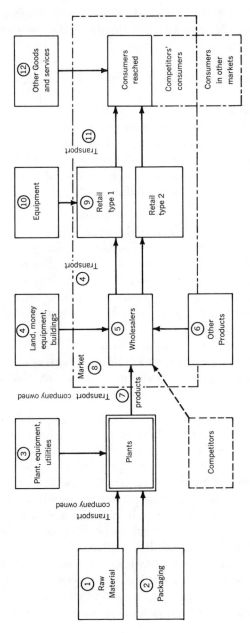

FIGURE 2.1 Flow diagram of a food business and scenario topics extracted from it. *Scenario topics:* (1) Produce raw material; (2) produce packaging; (3) build plants & manufacture equipment; (4) wholesaler services; (5) wholesaling; (6) other products for wholesalers; (7) extend current product line; (8) foreign markets; (9) retailing; (10) equipment for retailers; (11) home delivery; (12) entertainment.

7. It could expand its current product line into a number of closely related products not currently distributed by its wholesalers.

8. It could expand into foreign markets.

9. It could go into retailing, but this is precluded for legal reasons.

10. It could provide equipment used by its retailers.

11. It could go into the home-delivery business.

12. Since its principal products are normally consumed on social and recreational occasions, and since the company's advertising involves it extensively in entertainment, the business of providing recreation and entertainment is a possibility.

This procedure for selecting topics for scenarios is appropriate for companies that would consider only what might be called organic diversification; that is, diversification that involves continued use of what they consider to be their distinctive competence. Therefore such a procedure would not be appropriate for conglomerates. However, there is no restriction on how topics for scenarios can be selected; it is possible to devise a procedure that is appropriate to each situation.

Obtaining agreement on the areas to be developed into scenarios is only one step in the preparatory work. The other steps are reflected in the following suggested organization of the introductory section of the report ultimately to be prepared:

1. *Background*: a description of what scenarios are, what they are used for, and how this use fits into the total planning process.

2. *Possible futures for the company*: development of pessimistic, realistic, and optimistic reference projections for the company over the planning period; making explicit the assumptions and methods used in obtaining these projections. A wishful projection (however tentative) should also be prepared and compared with the reference projections. The gap to be filled by planning should be specified and its implications explored.

3. *Stylistic constraints*: general stylistic constraints, formulated by managers, that can be used in limiting the businesses to be considered in scenarios. For example, in a recent effort of this type the involved managers formulated such contraints as the following:

a. The company is not interested in any business that is government regulated.

b. The business into which it would go must permit entry with only modest initial investment but eventually permit large investments to be made.

c. The technology of any new business should be related to that used in its current business.

4. *Selection of scenario subjects*: the process described above or a substitute for it should be explained.

The scenarios themselves should be from 10 to 20 (double-spaced) typewritten pages in length. There are no hard-and-fast rules for their preparation, but I have found it convenient to organize each scenario into three sections.

1. In the first section, *Background,* the area involved is defined and certain possible businesses are excluded from consideration by using the previously formulated stylistic constraints.

2. In the second section, *Foreground,* a description is provided of what the relevant future is likely to be like. This is a reference projection and is usually based on materials culled from available literature.

3. In the third section, *The Company in 19– –,* a description is drawn of what the company might look like at the specified time and how it might get from where it is to the state described. This section is the heart of the scenario.

Once the scenarios are prepared the senior executives and managers of the company should read and discuss them. They may, and usually do, prefer a future that combines some of the features of several of the scenarios. An appropriate new "composite" scenario should then be prepared. This process should be continued until consensus on a preferred future is reached. (It should be made clear to those involved that later information may lead them to subsequent revision of this scenario.) The final scenario can then be used as a setting against which the planning process can be carried out.

Now let us consider formulation of performance objectives and goals.

PERFORMANCE OBJECTIVES AND GOALS

Definition

Most companies have formulated a statement of their performance objectives. They have learned through experience that these statements usually have little inspirational, let alone instructional, value. The futility of most formulations of objectives derives from the fact that they are not operationally meaningful. For example, it is common for companies to declare themselves to be for improved employee relations or morale. Such a statement provides no guidance because it does not provide a way of determining one's degree of success in pursuit of the objective. Yet it is possible to formulate such an objective operationally by asking how one could determine whether poor employee relations actually did exist. In most cases an answer to this question would reveal that three criteria would be used:

1. The greater the *attrition rate* of employees, the lower their morale. Attrition can be measured by the percentage of employees that voluntarily leave the company per year. Attrition is undesirable because it involves the costs of hiring, training, breaking in, and separation. Therefore minimization of these attrition-produced costs can be taken as an objective. A measure of attrition reduction can be used as an index of the reduction of the relevant costs.

2. The greater the *absenteeism* of employees, the lower their morale. This can be measured by the average percentage of employees absent per day. Absenteeism also involves a set of costs arising from lost production or substitution of personnel. Here too the underlying objective seems to be cost minimization, an index for progress toward which is the average percentage of employees absent per day.

3. The less the *productivity* of employees, the lower their morale. Productivity is more difficult to measure than attrition and absenteeism, but it is measurable. Its measurement involves the cost of direct labor per unit of output of acceptable quality. Cost minimization is obviously involved here as well.

Note that a more general objective—minimization of operating costs—includes each of these components of employee morale. To assert this is not to dehumanize the concept because reduction of the costs associated with poor morale requires deep understanding of the needs, wants, and satisfactions of the involved personnel. These costs cannot be reduced without dealing with problems of alienation, identification, involvement, and so on.

It is apparent that the operationally meaningful components of employee morale can be identified, defined, and measured. The same is true for even less "tangible" objectives. For example, one company has as one of its objectives, "to maintain the public's image of its products." To make this objective meaningful "image" must be operationally defined and made measurable. At first glance "image" may seem to be nothing but "market share," but this company's executives felt that a product with a good image but excessively high price could have only a small share of the market. This suggested that "image" means the share of the market that a product would have if there were no difference in price between the alternative products. Image in this sense can be measured by use of available marketing-research techniques. This variable is important because it is through changes in image that advertising, and to a certain extent pricing, affects share of the market.

Resolving Conflict between Objectives

Companies frequently formulate objectives that, at least under some circumstances, are not compatible; for example, they may want to simultaneously provide customers with better service and to minimize the costs of doing business (and hence of providing service). In some situations profit and market share cannot be increased simultaneously. Unless a way of resolving conflicts arising from the pursuit of such objectives is provided, managers cannot help but become anxious and frustrated in their vain efforts to cope with the conflicting pressures that are brought to bear on them. Under these circumstances their attempts to cope may not be in the company's best interests.

If measures applied to different objectives are made along the same scale, or if measures made along one scale can be transformed into measures along another, such conflicts can be resolved by formulating a higher level objective expressed on that scale.

"Profit" is often used in the formulation of such a higher level objective. We examine the use of this concept below.

A number of techniques are available for transforming measures obtained on one scale into values on another. These are discussed in some detail in Ackoff (1962, Chapter 3). An example here, however, may help.

A merchandising firm receives mail orders for goods selected by customers from a catalogue. The orders are filled by clerks who draw the required goods from stock, then package and mail them. The company wanted to determine how large a staff of order clerks it should maintain. Two objectives were involved: the company desired to minimize (*a*) the cost of its order-filling operations and (*b*) the time that customers wait to receive the ordered goods. A research team directed its efforts to resolving this conflict of objectives by transforming the negative value of a delay in delivery into a cost.

First records were examined to determine what proportion of orders were returned to the company by the customer because of delay and how this proportion varied with length of delay in receipt of goods by the customer. This analysis revealed a relationship like that shown in Figure 2.2; that is, delays of up to a few days had practically no effect on the return rate, but for increasing delays the proportion of returns increased at a relatively constant rate up to a point. Beyond that point the return rate remained relatively constant, rising almost imperceptibly.

Next an analysis was performed to determine whether the value of the goods was in any way related to the delay in shipping. No

FIGURE 2.2   Relationship between delivery delay and orders returned by customer.

FIGURE 2.3   Expected cost of returns as a function of delay in delivery.

relationship was found. This meant that the length of delay in shipping did not depend on the size or the value of an order.

The research team looked next at the cost of a returned order. This cost involved both direct outlays and customer dissatisfaction. Hence an analysis was made of the shipping cost and the salvage value of returned orders. Salvage value was expressed as a percentage of the price and was found to be relatively constant.

By studying the distribution of the sizes of orders it was then possible to determine the average dollar loss resulting from a returned order. To this expected cost was added the cost of shipping itself. Finally by multiplying this combined cost of a return by the probability of return a relationship like that shown in Figure 2.3 was obtained. This provided a transformation of delay time into costs.

The question remained as to whether or not customers were lost by long delays and consequently whether loss of future sales also had to be taken into account. It was found, however, that delays of the duration and frequency actually experienced by customers did not affect the amount or frequency of their orders. Therefore the transformation described above could be used without adjustment for loss of future business. It was very likely of course that repeated delays of long duration would affect future business, but the range of delays within which the company was willing to operate made the possibility of long delays very slight. If the situation had been otherwise and customers could have been lost due to delay, it would have been a more difficult, but by no means impossible, problem to convert the loss of customers into a cost.

It is not always possible to obtain as objective a transformation as that just described. Management's judgment is frequently required. But even in such cases research can considerably reduce the complexity of the necessary judgments. Consider, for example, an electric utility that wanted to minimize simultaneously its costs of operation and the number of deprivations of current that their customers had to endure. Here too the objectives were in conflict. It was possible for an operations-research team to determine the minimum annual operating cost for each of a wide variety of policies with respect to the maximum allowable number and duration of shortages. The managers were thus exposed to the cost consequences of each service policy. With this information available they had no great difficulty in selecting the combination of costs and deprivations that they considered to be most desirable.

Transformation of objectives into a common scale enables us to formulate more general objectives. Not only does this make it possible for us to resolve conflicts between low-level objectives but it enables us better to understand and evaluate alternative courses of action.

If, for example, we ask a carpenter at work, "What are you doing?" he could answer, "Putting some pieces of wood together," or "Putting up a door frame," or "Building a house." All three are his objectives, but each is formulated at a different level of generality. Means and ends are relative concepts, and hence every end is a means to a more general performance objective. To plan effectively it is necessary, but not sufficient, to understand the organization's performance objectives at a very high level of generality.

Very General Objectives

A course of action that produces a desired state (an objective) may also have consequences that are not expressed in the formulation of the particular objective. Men and organizations always pursue multiple objectives. Therefore in order to know whether the consequences of a course of action are desirable we require knowledge of the entire range of relevant objectives. The higher the level at which objectives are formulated, the more inclusive they are likely to be. We can better evaluate the carpenter's behavior if, in addition to knowing that he is trying to build a frame for a door, we also know that he is trying to build a house.

Formulations of corporate objectives are sometimes made at too low a level of generality. This frequently results in rejections of parts of a plan or all of it for no apparent reason. But there may be a good reason, and it may lie in a more generally formulated objective than that examined by the planners.

It is commonly assumed that "profit" or "profitability" maximization is a completely general formulation of a corporation's objectives ("profit" being the excess of revenues over costs and "profitability" being a measure of return on resources employed). This is not correct. First note that many profit(ability)-maximization possibilities are never considered for *stylistic* reasons. Furthermore, as many have noted, "profit(ability)" is seldom well defined (e.g., see Ansoff, 1965, Chapter 3, and Churchman, 1961, Chapter 3).

In a sense profit(ability) is a figment of the accountant's imagination. By changing one's accountant or accounting system profit(ability) can be destroyed or created. Therefore profit(ability) is not a matter of pure fact; it is a matter of financial and accounting policy. To be "for profit(ability)" is no more meaningful than to be "for virtue" without spelling out what virtue is.

Moreover, if profit(ability) is not defined, the consequences can be serious. For example, one large corporation showed annual operating losses for over two decades. The shareholders decided that this was not entirely uncontrollable and hence replaced the president. In his "inaugural address" the new president promised that the company would show a profit in his first full year of office, and it did. For that year no equipment was replaced no matter how bad it was; no maintenance was done except the minimum required to keep the equipment running; telephone calls, travel, and the use of supplies and outside services were cut to the bone. During his second year in office the president had to negotiate a merger in order to avoid bankruptcy.

Obviously most of us would say that this company's behavior was inexcusable because profit was not determined correctly: future costs incurred in that year should have been taken into account. But how should such costs—or, for that matter, future earnings—be taken into account? How should lost opportunities be accounted for? What is a rational discounting factor? Unless questions like these about profit, return on investment, or earnings, are answered explicitly in operationally meaningful terms, such statements as "We want to increase profit (or return in investment, or earnings) by X percent per year" are not very helpful.

Analysis of Profit(ability)

Such questions as have been raised above are very difficult to answer, but it becomes easier to do so if we convert profit(ability) into a set of operationally defined goals. We can make this conversion by use of a trivial equation:

$$\text{profit} = \text{gain} - \text{loss}$$

or

$$\text{profitability} = \frac{\text{gain} - \text{loss}}{\text{investments}}.$$

Goal formulation can begin by assuming that the major performance objective of any organization is either to

$$\text{maximize } (\text{gain} - \text{loss})$$

or to

$$\text{maximize } \frac{\text{gain} - \text{loss}}{\text{investment}}.$$

These statements are too general to have much meaning; yet they provide a basis for operationally meaningful goal formulation. Analysis of "gain" and "loss" can yield such a formulation. The analysis consists of "exploding" these concepts into a set of equations that identify their components and the *causal connections* among them. This process is illustrated in some detail in the following development of a "gain equation" for a particular brand of beer. Here "gain" can be defined as "income per year," and this can be exploded as follows:

Income per year =
1. Population of the market ×
2. Population-adjustment factor ×
3. Average discretionary income ×
4. Average percentage of discretionary income spent on food ×

5. Average percentage of amount spent on food that is spent on beverages ×
6. Average percentage of amount spent on beverages that is spent on alcoholic beverages ×
7. Average percentage of amount spent on alcoholic beverages that is spent on beer ×
8. Average percentage of amount spent on beer that is spent on relevant brand.

Before explaining how such an equation can be used in planning it should be noted that, if a company has more than one product line, one such equation should be prepared for each. At a lower level of the organization, where more detailed planning is done, similar equations should be prepared for each product, package size, and market area.

Now to examine this equation and its use. First the equation should be evaluated for a number of previous years; the further back, the better. By doing so one can determine where previous growth or contraction has come from and the sensitivity of income to each factor.

In the case at hand it is apparent that sale of beer depends on the size of the population in the relevant market (item 1); but it does not increase at the same rate as population does because beer consumption depends only on the *adult* population. Furthermore different age and sex groups in the adult population have significantly different rates of consumption, and these have changed over time. These and related facts that are revealed by historical analysis should be used in development of an appropriate population-adjustment factor (item 2).

How much money people can spend on beer depends on how much they have to spend. But not all of their income is available for such purchases. This suggests that disposable, rather than gross, income be used. A major portion of disposable income, however, is devoted to necessities, and most consumers do not consider beer to be a necessity. It is a "discretionary" product. It is not surprising, therefore, that changes in beer sales are more closely related to changes in discretionary income than to those in any other type of income.

The relationship between discretionary income and the percentage of it spent on food is not a simple one. The amount spent on food increases with this type of income, but only up to a point, at which it begins to level off. Rapid changes in the distribution of discretionary income have significantly affected beer sales in the past and can be expected to do so in the future.

The percentage of food expenditures that is allocated to beverages also depends on income but is not "linearly" related to it. At income levels at which increases in food expenditures slow down expenditures on beverages do not do the same.

Per capita consumption of alcohol was remarkably stable for several decades but recently increased significantly. Unless the reason for this increase is known one cannot reliably forecast such consumption in the future. Analysis revealed that such consumption is significantly related to discretionary income.

Alcoholic beverages fall into three classes: liquors, wines, and beers. The percentage of alcohol consumption that falls in each of these classes has varied over time and has even undergone significant changes in trend. Here too explanation is required. In this case the explanation was found to lie in a combination of economic, social, physiological, and technological variables. Some of these are subject to at least partial control by the company, and hence such analysis reveals some of the variables for which policies have to be planned.

Finally brand share changes over time and this too must be understood. To do so requires development of a marketing model that takes into account pricing, promotion, advertising, sales effort, and point-of-sales displays—and of course the behavior of competitors. (Such models are considered in more detail in the next chapter.)

As we work our way down the gain equation the terms are subject to increasing control. Use of such an equation to analyze the past often has the unpleasant consequence of revealing that most of the increases in income that a company has enjoyed are due to factors over which they have had no control. If this is true, it is important to know. The equation, however, makes possible increased control in the future.

Note that the gain equation provides a way of evaluating alternative markets into which the company can expand its sales; that is, a gain equation can be developed for each potential or actual market area, and this provides a basis for comparing them, particularly if relevant costs are taken into account. For example, if consideration is given to entering a state in which a brand has not previously been sold, gain can be estimated for that state by use of historical data plus an estimate of the market share that would be obtained if entry were made. In order to obtain such an estimate it is necessary to have a model that relates market share to the relevant characteristics of the market and the way the brand is to be introduced and marketed in that area. Such models have been developed. They include such policy variables as timing and amount of advertising, pricing, and retail coverage.

The most important effect that development of gain and loss equations has on planning is that it forces search for *explanation*. For example, explanatory market-share models, as noted above, can be developed. Such models (for consumables) can sometimes be constructed by using only three types of variable:

1. *Product image*: the average percentage of purchases by consumers that would go to the brand if all brands were equally priced at the average of the current prices of these brands. (This variable can be estimated by experimental or questionnaire techniques.)

2. *Brand loyalty*: the rate of change in percentage of purchases of a brand as its price changes while all other prices remain fixed at the average current price. (This variable can also be estimated by experimental or questionnaire techniques.)

3. *Actual prices* of the competing brands.

Once such an explanatory model has been constructed, it is possible to go further and develop models to explain *image* and *brand loyalty* in terms of advertising and distribution variables.

Gain and loss equations make possible better forecasts than can usually be obtained from descriptive equations alone; and, together with associated models of each term, they make possible the evaluation of alternative policies and even suggest some that should be evaluated.

Corresponding cost equations for each product line should also be constructed and analyzed. These equations should reflect not the accounting system but the process in which costs are incurred. A detailed flow diagram of the process helps in identifying the relevant costs and their interactions. Therefore each term in a cost equation should be associated with an identifiable set of decisions or actions by the organization.

Once the gain and cost equations have been constructed, we should forecast for each year in the planning period the value of each term over which the company has no control. The other terms can be affected by what the company does and therefore have to be "set." To do so is to specify the company's goals. Whether or not the goals that have been set can be attained or surpassed cannot be determined until policies and practices have been selected and evaluated, and resource requirements have been taken into account; that is, until other aspects of planning have been considered. Hence these goals may be "set" several times before they are finally "settled."

When the goals have been set, the gains and losses can be estimated and aggregated over existing product lines for each year in the planning period. If this aggregated figure falls short of what the company desires and if it represents the best that the company can expect to do, the difference between what is expected and what is desired specifies what must be provided by new products or services. The consensus scenario specifies the nature of the products or services that should then be considered. Once new products or services have been added, their gain and loss equations should also be developed and analyzed.

If a performance objective has been transformed onto a monetary scale or if its contribution to a more general performance objective that is expressed in monetary terms has been specified, it can be incorporated into gain or loss equations. If this has not been done, judgment is required to choose among the possible combinations of attainment levels of noncombinable objectives. But, as we have noted, the cost and/or gain consequences of different levels of an untransformed objective can facilitate the effective use of judgment.

SUMMARY

Planning is based on (a) a *reference projection*—a prediction of what is likely to come about if there is no planned intervention; and (b) a *wishful projection*—an expression of where the company would like to be at the end of the planning period. The objective of planning is to produce a *planning projection* that specifies how far the planners believe the organization can go toward fulfilling its wishes.

Desired states or outcomes are *objectives*. *Goals* are objectives that are scheduled for attainment during the period planned for. Objectives are of two types, *stylistic* and *performance*. Stylistic objectives are valued for their own sake; performance objectives are valued instrumentally. Stylistic objectives can be formulated by use of *scenarios*, which are qualitative descriptions of what the company might be at some specified time in the future. These enable an organization's management to reach consensus on the kind of business it would like to be in and the way (style) in which it would like to conduct it.

Performance objectives require operational definition; that is, specification of the means by which progress toward attainment of such objectives can be measured. Potential conflicts between porformance objectives can be resolved by transforming their relevant measures onto one common scale, usually monetary. Analysis of actual performance often makes such transformations possible. Objectives that have been so transformed can be combined into a more general objective. The more general the level of formulation, the less likely are planners to overlook significant consequences of decisions.

Profit maximization is commonly taken to be the most general formulation of a company's performance objectives. But profit is often ill defined. It can be operationally defined and transformed into goals by constructing gain and loss equations for each product line, for each year in the planning period. In these equations gains and losses are broken down into the factors that produce them. The research and analysis required to develop such equations yields valuable understanding of how the system being planned for operates, and it identifies the controllable variables that should be treated in the part of the planning process that is discussed in the next chapter.

It is apparent that one cannot fix goals until at least the means to be employed in pursuing them have been considered. This emphasizes the point made earlier that all parts of a plan are interdependent. Unfortunately we can only discuss them one at a time. We turn now to a consideration of the means to be employed.

Chapter 3

POLICIES AND COURSES OF ACTION

INTRODUCTION

Means, like ends, can be formulated at different levels of generality. In order of increasing generality there are *courses of action, practices, procedures, programs,* and *policies.*

Course of action: a particular act of a person or group; for example, hiring a particular person, making a particular purchase, or moving to a particular location.

Practice: a course of action that is repeated under similar circumstances; for example, running a sale before a particular holiday each year or hiring only college graduates to fill certain jobs.

Procedure: a sequence of actions directed at a single (usually short-run) goal that is repeatedly pursued; for example, hiring, purchasing, or billing procedures.

Program: an ordered set of interrelated actions, generally more complex than a procedure, directed toward a specific (usually long-run) objective that is pursued only once; for example, a diversification or building program.

Policy: a rule for selecting a course of action, a decision rule; for example, "fill orders on a first-come, first-served basis" or "do not permit any competitor to undersell us."

For most of our purposes it is sufficient to distinguish between courses of action, taken separately or in combination, and policies, which are rules for selecting courses of action.

A proper policy is a rule that takes into account the relevant conditions that pertain at the time action is required. Policies, therefore, permit use of all the relevant information that is available at the time of decision. For this reason they provide more flexibility than do specified courses of action. Consequently planning should be concerned with courses of action only for the present, and with policies where action is required in the future. It is preferable, for example, to have a rule that specifies how purchase quantities should be determined at a particular time, rather than to specify that a fixed quantity is always to be purchased. Even where policies are established, however, it is necessary to forecast over the planning period the values of the variables that are relevant to its use. Otherwise the policy cannot be evaluated nor can the resource requirements that it generates be estimated.

The evaluation of alternative courses of action is a preoccupation of many planners. Unfortunately this preoccupation frequently precludes their involvement in what is often a more fruitful activity: *inventing, designing,* or otherwise *creating new* alternative courses of action or policies. Once one understands the limitations of available alternatives, it is often possible to develop new ones that are so obviously superior to those previously available that comparative evaluation is hardly necessary. Creation of new courses of action and policies—rather than evaluation of old ones —is a key to successful planning. Therefore the emphasis in the discussion that follows is often on examples involving such innovation.

The matter can be put another way. It is usually much better to *dissolve* a problem than it is to solve it. Dissolution of a problem requires innovation, whereas it solution requires only evaluation. Recall, for example, the case referred to in Chapter 1 in which a manufacturer of a raw material in more than 3000 different forms received small infrequent orders for each of a large number of these items. This resulted in a difficult production-scheduling problem. Rather than looking for the best method of scheduling production, a new incentive system for salesmen was designed to eliminate sales of most of the small-volume unprofitable items and significantly increase sales of large-volume profitable items. In this way the problem was dissolved rather than solved.

MODELS OF CHOICE

The key to both creating and evaluating courses of action and policies lies in *understanding* the system involved; that is, in the ability to *explain* its behavior, not merely to predict it. One may be able to predict the behavior of a system without being able to explain it, for example, by extrapolating from its past behavior. The ability to explain, however, necessarily involves the ability to predict. More important, it provides a basis for redesigning the system in some fundamental way so as either to eliminate problems or significantly improve effectiveness.

Research, which involves at least some limited experimentation, is usually required to develop understanding of most systems or even significant parts of them. The management scientist normally embodies his understanding, once acquired, in a model of the system involved; that is, in symbolic representations of the type discussed in Chapter 1. Such models can be used both to evaluate and innovate, but innovation generally requires broader understanding: the ability to explain and perceive the interrelatedness of parts of the system. Evaluative planning, therefore, is less demanding than is the innovative type. For example, a company that supplies a line of several thousand related products used in a wide variety of manufacturing processes experienced a growth in inventory several times that of its sales volume. All of its production takes place in one plant, which supplies more than 100 distribution warehouses located in major metropolitan areas in the United States. Customers either pick up supplies from these warehouses or delivery is made from the warehouses to them.

A model of the production-inventory-supply system was developed by a research team. The measure of performance that was used in the model was "total cost per year." The controlled variables were (*a*) the size and frequency of production runs for each product in the line and (*b*) the size and frequency of orders placed on the factory by the warehouses. The uncontrolled variables included the usual costs and total customer demand per product type per unit time. The model was solved and yielded significant but unimpressive improvements in the system. Management felt that further reductions were possible. Hence a second research group was asked to examine the work of the first.

The second group systematically checked the model and the estimates of the values of the uncontrolled variables that appeared in it. No errors were found, but one characteristic of demand caught its attention. Most orders placed on the warehouses were for very small quantities. When the researchers asked why, they learned that the products deteriorated under normal storage conditions. The company's warehouses were air conditioned to prevent such deterioration. Hence consuming manufacturers who could not store the material properly maintained only a few days' supply of the products.

Analysis of the model showed that a very large portion of the inventory was required because of the variability of demand over short periods of time. The variability of demand was found to derive from the fact that most individual orders were for small quantities. It seemed clear, however, that the size of customers' orders could not be changed significantly, thereby reducing uncertainty of demand. But there is another characteristic of orders that the researchers identified, one which did not appear explicitly in the model but which had a considerable effect on inventory size: the amount of time between a customer's placing an order and delivery. Orders were normally filled "immediately." However, it was clear that, if all orders were placed, say, a year ahead of time, the company could produce and stock to order, no matter how small the quantities picked up by, or delivered to, customers. Use of the model showed that the reductions in inventory that were theoretically obtainable with long lead time were dramatic. Therefore the research team took its problem to be one of increasing the lead time that customers gave the warehouses in filling their orders.

The research team used the model to calculate how much lead time was worth to the company and then designed a pricing system that reflected this value; the longer the lead time given by a customer, the lower the price. Prices were set to allow the customers and the company to share the reduction of inventory costs. The system was installed and produced large reductions in inventory. It turned out that the customers' purchasing agents generally knew their companys' production schedules (and hence requirements for the products involved) about a month in advance and therefore could give several weeks' lead time on the average. They never had done so because there had been no advantage to their sharing this information with the supplier.

Models Required

Ideally the scientific planner would like to have one model that represents and explains the entire system and its environment. However, he is not yet able to construct such comprehensive models. At best he can only construct models of parts or aspects of the system and sometimes link these together in a way that approximates an overall model. It is important, therefore, that we know how to divide a business system into parts that can be modeled to at least some extent. One way of doing so is as follows:

1. *The firm.* Some conception of what a firm does and can do is obviously required if we are to plan for it.

2. *Supply.* Some understanding is required of the system that provides the firm with the required materials, equipment, facilities, and services.

3. *Distribution and sales.* This is the system that transmits the output of the firm to the ultimate consumer. In some cases this system may be part of the firm, but in most cases some independently operated businesses are involved in these processes (e.g., wholesalers or retailers).

4. *Consumers.* Unless the nature and reasons for consumption of the firm's products are understood, effecting planning for the future cannot be carried out.

5. *Competition.* The ability to predict competitive behavior is obviously required in the development of both tactics and strategy.

6. *Environment.* The dynamics of the environment must be understood and forecast in order to plan effectively. The economic, social, political, and technological aspects of the environment (i.e., the larger system that contains the firm) should also be taken into account.

Now let us consider in more detail these six aspects of a business system and the state of the art and science of modeling each of them.

Models of the Firm

We can seldom represent in a single model the relationships among all the variables controlled by a firm. It is usually necessary to construct separate models of at least each major function—such as purchasing, maintenance, production, and distribution—and to connect them into an approximate representation of the whole. The art and science of modeling are not equally advanced in each functional area. Functions with a large "human" component— such as marketing, research and development, and personnel—are much more difficult to model than those that are primarily machine based or consist of numerous small repetitive actions or decisions. Various aspects of purchasing, production, distribution, transportation, and finance are relatively easy to model, and in general, models of these functions can be linked to approximate a model of the whole. The construction of models, even in well-understood areas, consumes considerable time and effort, more than those charged with the responsibility for planning can usually devote to such activity. Therefore effective planning must be built on a foundation of continuing management research. For example, it often takes longer to develop an adequate model of a marketing function than it does to develop a long-range plan. Planning should not be delayed while waiting for good models to be provided by the management sciences; nor should the development of adequate management science activities await the initiation of planning.

A manager is unlikely to be aware of how little understanding he has of some of the operations for which he is responsible. Planning tends to bring such deficiencies into consciousness but seldom can itself provide the opportunity for removing them. For example, few firms have a rational basis for setting their advertising expenditures. They do not know what the effect of such expenditures is on their income. Advertising budgets are usually set almost mechanically as a fixed percentage of expected sales. Media selection, timing, and selection of messages are seldom based on anything firmer. If one knows no better, one may have to assume that sales are related to advertising in the way they have been assumed to be in the past, but planning makes one aware of such an assumption and its potential costliness.

As a result of planning Anheuser-Busch, Inc. launched advertising research in 1962. Within six years it had at least partial understanding of the effect of each controllable aspect of advertising on sales. This enabled the company to reduce its advertising expenditures per unit sold by more than half and simultaneously to enjoy the most rapid growth of any company in its industry. In an area in which little is known even a little understanding can go a very long way (see Vogel, 1969).

Not all the models that a planner would like to have available are likely to be available to him. Nevertheless he must go ahead with whatever he has and make his plan depend as much as possible on what understanding is available, and as little as possible on folklore. In many instances planners must use managers' judgments as a basis for planning. However, they can direct research to these judgments and build into the plan a capability for self-modification in light of the results of such research. For example, in a long-range plan prepared for the Lamp Division of the General Electric Company (Glover and Ackoff, 1956) it was necessary to determine how many sales calls would be required to obtain specified sales goals. Arbitrary decisions were made on the basis of previous average sales obtained per call made. But a study of the question was initiated as soon as the plan was completed (see Waid, Clark, and Ackoff, 1956). This study made it possible to revise the plan a year later, reducing the manpower requirements as a basis for planning. However, they can direct research of new accounts obtained. (This case is discussed in more detail in Chapter 4 in the section on Personnel Planning).

Models of Supply

It is not uncommon for firms to assume, even implicitly, that there will always be enough raw material and other required supplies at an acceptable price. Sometimes this leads to lack of anticipation of major changes in the "supply picture." In an age of rapid technological change modification of this "picture" is not at all uncommon. For example, the market for a particular variety of a grain lies almost exclusively in one industry because another variety has replaced it for most other types of consumption. To farmers the substitute is more profitable than the older variety. The industry is now in a precarious supply situation, one that could have been detected a number of years ago by study of the dynamics of their suppliers' markets. It is much harder to find corrective measures today than it would have been a few years ago.

On the other hand, the correct anticipation of the substitution of transistors for vacuum tubes not only changed existing businesses but also made possible the creation of profitable new ones (e.g., miniaturized radios, television sets, and tape recorders).

In short, a firm should have some understanding of the markets in which it operates as a consumer. Perception of impending changes in these markets and its suppliers' activities can indicate either the need for research and development, acquisition of sources of supply, redesign of old products, or design of new ones.

If a firm's consumption of a material, product, or service is a large part of total consumption, it is apparent that the possibility of self-supply, if not supply to others, should be given serious consideration.

Distribution and Sales Links

Most firms, but not all, use links not entirely under their control to carry their output to the ultimate consumer. These links may include other manufacturers, brokers, wholesalers, agents, retailers, and so on. The costs of distribution and sales associated with these links have increased rapidly, and in many cases the nature and organization of these channels have changed radically in recent years. Distribution and marketing have been significantly affected by social, economic, and technological changes, and can be expected to continue to be so affected. Planners should try to picture changes that might take place, assess their significance to the firm, and consider ways in which they might be exploited. For example, the following is a passage from a preliminary planning document prepared for a company that produces a line of food products that I shall refer to as "X."

"There is no doubt that traffic on city streets will increase in the immediate future. Both the number of automobiles and trucks and the average use they will get will increase more rapidly than street capacity. Therefore travel by car in metropolitan areas will take longer and be more unpleasant. This will result in fewer shopping trips with larger amounts purchased per trip.

"There are other, and perhaps more important, forces pushing in the same direction. Average income will continue to increase and bring with it more and larger dwelling units, refrigerators, and freezers, thereby providing more food-storage space in the home. This too will encourage fewer and larger shopping trips.

"More women will have college educations and engage in professional careers and community services after marriage. Servants will be more costly and harder to find. This will force women to do more shopping in the evenings and reduce the frequency of their shopping. It will also increase demand for convenience stores and willingness to pay for the convenience. Although the cost of food will rise there is clear indication that food in the future will take a smaller percentage of the increasing income, and therefore women will be willing to pay more for convenience and service.

"Automobiles are likely to become smaller. Small urban automobiles are already being produced by Westinghouse and others. Ford, General Motors, and Chrysler are known to be rushing development of similar cars. Use of small two- and four-passenger cars is likely to be accelerated by the growing air-pollution problem, and incentives in the form of reduced taxes and license fees are likely to be provided by the government so that public expenditures for streets can be kept from growing.

"The small car will be coming into vogue just as women are decreasing the frequency of their shopping trips and increasing the amount purchased per trip. The cars will be too small to carry all that is purchased.

"For these reasons, then, we can expect an increase in home delivery. But these are not the only reasons.

"Length of life is increasing. More and more senior citizens will be around enjoying their retirement in the future, many living in specially designed neighborhoods and communities. Such communities are already increasing. With larger retirement benefits they will buy more but will be less inclined or able physically to handle large purchases. Here too an increased demand for home delivery will arise.

"It is already technically possible to phone a store and put one's order into an automated order-taker by code. The video phone and closed-circuit television—both already in operation—will make it possible for the woman in the house or out of it to see what she is buying, even in color. She will be able to scan the shelves and displays of a store without leaving her desk. Naturally she will expect delivery of what she orders in this way.

"Reaching out a little further into the future it is not at all unlikely that a computer will keep a record of a household's purchases and analyze them to determine what it will need when, and deliver without an order being placed. This is already being done by heating-fuel distributors, and much less is spent on fuel than is spent on food.

"O.K.; so there is going to be an increase in home delivery. But we do not know how it will be provided and when. We can wait and see and adapt to it when it comes or we can find out how to make something of it and out of it. As a minimum it offers us an opportunity to reduce out-of-stock of X at home. As a maximum it offers us an exciting and potentially profitable direction for relevant diversification and expansion. Note that the service industry is already the most rapidly growing industry in the United States. Are we going to be on the serving or receiving end of things?"

It is clear that how one views the possibilities of fruitful change in sales and distribution depends to a large extent on the concept one has of the consumer.

Models of the Consumer

Few companies understand *why* their products are consumed, although they think they do. Companies believe their own advertising much more than their consumers do. Most companies comfortably assume that their consumers are irrational and therefore are satisfied to seek the nature and source of this assumed irrationality. Few companies are willing to consider the alternative possibility that at least in the long run consumption tends to be rational and that irrationality is much more a characteristic of the supplier than of the consumer. Yet experience has shown this to be a much more productive approach to planning. E. H. Vogel, when Vice President of Marketing at Anheuser-Busch, Inc., put it this way (1969, pp. 21–22):

"Consumer marketing problems are not solved by assuming the consumer is irrational and the marketer is rational, *but just the opposite*.

"Consumers may behave irrationally in the short run, but not in the long run. They learn fast. Marketers who claim consumers are irrational really mean that they do not understand consumers and either don't know how to acquire such understanding or don't want to. Now mind you, I am not saying consumers are conscious of what they are doing or why. They can be rational even if they don't understand themselves. It is our job to find out why they do what they do, even if they don't know. . . .

"One brief and familiar example. Most marketers of gasoline assume consumers buy on the basis of brand preferences. Policies based on this assumption have uniformly failed. Studies have shown that most consumers do not have gasoline brand preferences, and for good reason: they can't tell the difference between the performances of competing brands. And again for good reason: there isn't any significant difference between them. It turns out, however, that consumers pick service stations, not brands, and they do so in such a way as to minimize the amount of time they lose in buying gasoline. This is completely rational behavior under the circumstances. A gasoline marketer who knows and uses this information can select his sites and design his stations so as to give him a significant competitive advantage. In our work we have found that consumer preferences for different kinds of alcoholic beverages are not irrational but are based on different functions that different beverages perform well under different environmental, economic, and physiological conditions.

"We must not only develop understanding of the consumer and do so by at least starting with the assumption that he is rational, but we must also start with the assumption that most of our marketing errors and failures are due to our own irrationality. . . .

"To become rational and effective marketers we must come to understand each aspect of marketing: advertising, pricing, sales effort (manpower), and point-of-sales displays and communications. Understanding means knowing what causes produce what effects.

"For example, in general the more advertising a company does, the larger are its sales. It is commonly assumed therefore that to sell more one must advertise more. This is irrational for two reasons. First most companies set their advertising budgets as a fixed percentage of forecast sales. This means that increased forecasts cause increased advertising, not that increased advertising causes increased sales. Secondly, advertising is a stimulus and purchasing is a response. In psychology, where a great deal has been done on how responses relate to the amount of stimulation, no instance has been found in which responses increase linearly or even continuously with increases in stimulation.

"This irrationality is perpetuated by advertising agencies, and for good reason. Their income increases as advertising does. There is no more irrational way for marketers to pay advertising agencies. Can you imagine paying your auditor a percentage of the taxes you pay the government? Would you expect them, if so compensated, to minimize your tax bill? Do you begin to see now what I mean by the irrationality of the marketer?"

I once asked the manager of a packaged food business whose products have a high sugar content, "Why is the British per capita consumption of sugar so much higher than ours?" He answered, "Because they like it more than we do." I then asked, "How do you know this?" He replied, "They consume more of it, don't they?"

There is a good reason for the consumption of sugar, of which most of its consumers and many of its producers are unaware. The answer lies in the ratio of carbohydrate to protein intake and their effects on the blood-sugar level. The British consumption of these foods is in a ratio that differs from that of American consumption, and for good reason. This ratio affects the distribution of blood-sugar levels over time, and this distribution affects the need for sugar. The more protein consumed, the less the need for sugar.

With some understanding of this and related phenomena we can explain why the British, who consume more calories than Americans do, put on less weight; why soft drinks with sugar have a small adult market; why those with synthetic sweetners have found such a good market; and why a new adult market for sour soft drinks has been found in the United States.

Dramatic changes in a business can be suggested by an understanding of why people consume what they do, when they do, where they do. The suggestions may, of course, not be acceptable to management. For example, an automobile insurance company had been losing money because it had been issuing policies to more poor drivers (young unmarried males) than most companies do. Its managers were preoccupied with trying to find ways of attracting more good drivers and fewer bad ones. This way of approaching the problem assumes no knowledge of why accidents occur and hence of why the company was losing money.

Another way of looking at the same problem is to ask, How can bad drivers be converted into good ones? After all, the company had a very large share of the bad-driver market, and this is a large market. But to take such a question seriously commits one to finding out *why* accidents occur and *how* to convert bad drivers into better ones. Much of the required information is already available. For example, one important cause of accidents is the anonymity of the driver. Most of us are more aggressive, ruder, and less courteous behind a wheel than we are in face-to-face contacts with others. In a car we do not have to confront those we treat improperly; we can speed away, avert our eyes, or lag behind.

These facts suggest a possibility. Suppose the company were to agree to insure anybody who agrees to display his identity in a suitable way on the exterior of any car he drives. Furthermore, if he is the cause of an accident, he must add a special sign so indicating, and he must use this for six months. This would remove the driver's anonymity and give others a chance to keep their distance from those who have recently caused an accident. This suggestion overlaps in principle Britain's successful requirement that any car driven by a learner carry a special license plate with a large "L." The proposal was nevertheless rejected by the company.

Models of Competition

Models of competitors, where there are few of them, have been extensively developed. Economists have long been concerned with quantitative representation and prediction of restricted competition; that is, for duopolies and oligopolies. Therefore planners working in industries that can be so characterized have a substantial literature to go on. As the number of competitors increases, however, understanding them becomes more difficult. Even where we can model each competitor separately, the linkage between these models seldom enables us to reproduce, let alone forecast, competitive interactions. The situation is by no means hopeless, however, because we have learned that in many cases in which it is difficult to model competitors it is *not* difficult to model *competition*. This distinction is fine but critical.

Consider a company that obtains its business by submitting closed bids for contracts. It may be one of a dozen companies that can compete for such contracts. Management scientists may be able to construct models of each competitor with a great deal of effort and forecast which ones will do what in a specific situation.

This approach does not often yield usable results. However, the situation may be looked at in another way. In any past bidding situation only *one* bidder was important: the winner if "we" lost, and the closest bidder if "we" won. Clearly the identity of this "one" company changes from situation to situation, but this changing "it" constitutes the significant competition. What others did is at best of only peripheral interest. Now it turns out that competition, defined as the one other company whose behavior is of interest in each specific case, is often quite predictable. I have found it to be so in such diverse industrial and business settings as in bidding for rights to explore for oil and minerals, and in bidding for construction, fabrication, and service contracts.

In pricing, rather than bidding, it also frequently turns out that, although we may have difficulty in predicting how each competitor will respond to a change in our pricing, the relevant response (but not who will make it) is quite predictable. Responses to the introduction of new products or modifications of old ones are similarly predictable.

The use of an aggregated competitor to replace many competitors probably works best where competition is relatively unrestricted, where we have what P. J. D. Wiles (1967) calls a *free market*.

Advertising, of course, is a major instrument of competition. It tends to be used heavily where brand differences are either not perceptible or not significant if perceived. In such situations advertising is usually directed toward producing the illusion of brand superiority where it does not exist in fact. It is important in planning to determine whether such efforts actually do succeed and at what cost they succeed or fail; and to compare the use of advertising with other marketing tactics and strategies, particularly with the creation of a real brand difference. The likelihood that such a difference can be created depends greatly on how well the consumer and consumption are understood.

Understanding of consumers can frequently be expressed in a mathematical model that facilitates evaluation and design of alternative courses of action and policies; for example, when the amount of time lost in stopping at a gasoline service station was found to affect the percentage of passing cars that stopped for service, further research was able to establish how this percentage is affected by the driver's perception of lost time, how this perception relates to actual time lost, and how actual time lost is related to the route of the driver and the characteristics of the service station (e.g., number and location of pumps and attendants, and entrances and exits). Such understanding could be expressed in one mathematical model that made it possible to improve site selection for new stations, to design these stations so as to maximize sales at selected sites, and to redesign existing stations so as to increase their sales.

Models of the Environment

Planners are necessarily concerned with the broad social, economic, political, and technological context within which the firm will have to operate in the future. As I have already mentioned, the problem is less one of forecasting the future than it is one of perceiving what is virtually certain to occur, of determining how to exploit and possibly accelerate the "inevitable," and of taking credit for doing so. In this way a company does not merely have to adapt to changes as they occur, but it can help create the future and the opportunities that it can present.

Every company is concerned with the future and what it will bring. Some are only slightly concerned, because they feel secure in the belief that they can respond to whatever changes the future may bring and they can do well enough to at least survive. Others are greatly concerned with the future but for different reasons. One group feels that it is not enough to respond to changes *after* they have occurred; they want to prepare and be ready for the changes. These companies tend to be preoccupied with forecasting the future. Another and smaller group are not so much interested in forecasting the future as they are in creating it. For these the objective is not to predict but to control the future. Thus there are three attitudes toward the future, which, ordered from the most to the least prevalent are (a) wait and see, (b) predict and prepare, and (c) make it happen.

Those who benefit most from the future are those who have helped create it. One may be able to survive and even prosper without making the future, but one cannot *pull away from the pack* without doing so.

Unfortunately what is relatively certain about the future is seldom obvious. It only becomes so in retrospect. Fortunately, however, a great deal of attention by a number of competent people has been directed toward determining what is likely to happen in the future. There has been a rash of studies of the year 2000 (see, for example, Kahn and Wiener, 1967, and the Summer 1967 issue of *Daedalus*). These provide rich insights and sound ground from which to look at the future from the point of view of a particular firm. In addition much work has been done recently on the techniques of technological forecasting (see, for example, Jantsch, 1967).

A few examples may be helpful. In the process of developing a long-range plan for an appliance manufacturer attention was directed at the question, Why were appliances developed in their current form? That is, why had particular functions (e.g., cooking, food preservation, and dishwashing) been isolated and mechanized? Reconstruction of the past showed that appliances had emerged during a period in which consumers had little capital to invest in them, and hence designers had concentrated on mechanizing as few functions in combination as possible in order to produce low-cost units. However, examination of buying behavior in the current market revealed that two or more appliances were usually purchased simultaneously. Such purchases are usually associated with remodeling or a move. This suggested combining functions in general-purpose appliances. Analysis revealed considerable cost advantages in doing so. Generalization of this idea led to the design of a kitchen as an integrated unit, as a mechanized system. Such a "product" was developed and is currently available. The bathroom was similarly examined, with similar results.

The next stage involved combinations of rooms, the most attractive of which appeared to be a unit containing kitchen, bathroom, and utility room. Such units have also been made available.

Still further generalization led to consideration of the possibility of manufacturing a house, not prefabricating it, but manufacturing a complete unit. A study of future housing needs, distribution of income, and construction costs made the future market for such houses look quite attractive. It was also apparent, however, that many legal, social, and economic obstacles had to be overcome before such houses could be marketed successfully. The plan emerged with a transitional schedule from appliance manufacturing, through room manufacturing, to house manufacturing. It involved entry into the house-trailer business because the mobile home is already a manufactured unit that enjoys the largest share of the low-cost-housing market. This business provided a laboratory in which many of the problems of house manufacturing could be solved before entry into the normal house business.

One further generalization was made. The *community* itself was examined as a potential product. Analysis revealed the growth of a market for new communities and the possibility of considerable sales and profit for providing them. Within 10 years after completion of the plan the company involved is profitably engaged in each of these extensions of the appliance business and is becoming a major force in reshaping the rooms, houses, and communities in which we are and will be living.

In another planning study carried out in 1961 it was found that cities could not possibly add streets and highways at a rate that would maintain their then current levels of automobile traffic. It was felt that increased congestion would not be tolerable and therefore that one or both of two alternatives would have to be pursued: increase in mass transit or reduction in the size of the automobile. Further study of the consumer indicated that increased mass transit would not be acceptable to him because of the inconvenience and lack of comfort necessarily involved in its use. Therefore it was concluded that a small urban automobile was inevitable. The fact that automobiles in the city currently carry an average of only slightly more than one person led to the conclusion that a two-passenger (or at most a three-passenger) vehicle would serve most needs. It was found that by restricting the use of city streets during working hours to such vehicles existing city streets would enjoy an increase in capacity that could not be obtained by cities even if they were to spend all of their available funds on improving the current system. Add to this the growing threat of air pollution and out comes the recommendation that development of a small urban vehicle be made a planning goal. Today of course there is little prophesy left in predicting the emergence of such a vehicle.

Planners should keep the organizations for which they plan and their policies flexible where the future is uncertain and become relatively fixed only where there is relative certainty.

One good perception of an inevitability may be worth any amount of forecasting uncertainties. Such a perception can provide the pivot around which a new future for the firm can be made to revolve.

REINVENTING THE SYSTEM: IDEALIZED DESIGN

I have tried to show how understanding a system increases our ability to find innovative and superior courses of action and policies. However, even when equipped with such understanding we are frequently prevented from perceiving possibilities by our excessive familiarity with the existing system. Many of the constraints under which managers and researchers operate are not imposed from without, but are self-imposed. Policy innovation depends critically on our ability to bring these self-imposed constraints into question.

The most effective way of which I am aware for systematically reviewing such constraints and questioning their justification consists of engaging in the exercise of *reinventing* the system that is being planned for. To describe and illustrate the process I draw on some work being done on long-range planning for a university. I use this example because my own involvement with such institutions for more than 30 years puts me in much the same position with respect to them that most managers are in with respect to the businesses of which they are a part. (The following is extracted in modified form from Ackoff, 1968.) Before turning to the example let me consider some general aspects of the process involved.

One who attempts to improve an existing organization is very likely to be preoccupied with correcting relatively apparent deficiencies in details of its operations. A concept of the organization as an integrated system is essential if an improvement in one of its parts is to be kept from producing a compensating deficiency in another of its parts.

Even small corrective measures cannot be evaluated effectively unless one has a conception of what the organization *should* be like, as a *whole* and *ideally*. An idealized conception of an organization should consist of more than a set of unrelated or loosely related ideas; the ideas should be completely integrated into a cohesive system.

Equipped with an idealized concept we can systematically plan the transition of an existing organization toward one that we want. Without it we can only proceed in a piecemeal and ad hoc way, responding to current pressures not to long-run needs.

Therefore, it seems to me, one of the most practical things we can do in preparing ourselves for effective long-range strategic planning for an organization is to engage in the invention or design of an idealized form of that organization, an exercise that should ignore all apparently practical constraints. Once such a design has been completed, we can determine how closely it can be approximated and we can systematically plan the transition toward the ideal.

However, we should not engage in designing an ideal without awareness of two essential characteristics of such an effort. First, our concept of an ideal will change over time, and hence our formulation of it at any moment of time is at most a *relative absolute*. Second, since our efforts at idealization are necessarily rooted in our own culture, any ideal that we formulate is not likely to be ideal in societies other than the one in which we have grown. Therefore a formulation of an ideal is not only a relative absolute, it is also *absolutely relative*.

One final general point: I am certain that one essential characteristic of an ideal university or an ideal business is that it would be continuously redesigning itself and would use controlled experiments to evaluate at least the important features of the redesigns. Therefore, if idealized design is a utopian effort, it is utopian with a difference: the utopia involved is dynamic and far from perfect but is capable of systematic progress toward that elusive ultimate ideal, perfection.

In order to illustrate the process of idealized design I use one aspect of the redesigned pedagogy of the university.

We cannot predict accurately how many of each type of college graduate will be required a decade from now. Even if we could, we would still have the problem of allocating their "production" to individual institutions. Our ability to forecast manpower requirements in the future is not likely to improve because the rate of technological change will increase. This will augment an already considerable tendency of college graduates to switch fields; for example, W. G. Ireson (1959, p. 507) observed:

"The most important fact brought out by . . . surveys over a period of thirty years is that more than 60 percent of those persons who earned [engineering] degrees in the United States, either became managers of some kind within ten to fifteen years or left the engineering profession entirely to enter various kinds of business ventures."

Even when recent graduates remain in the field in which they were trained they will have to replace their obsolete college-acquired knowledge with what has taken its place if they are to maintain their effectiveness. For these reasons it is essential that college graduates be as flexible as possible, that they be motivated to continue their education after graduation, and that they know how to do so.

Therefore the underlying theme in this design is that *the objective of education is learning, not teaching.*

The things that ought to be learned by a university student are not all best learned in the same way. Therefore I have designed four different learning procedures, only one of which is presented here.

The best way for a student to learn a well-defined and recorded body of knowledge is to teach it to another.

This, it seems to me, is common knowledge among those who have taught. When a teacher instructs on material that is new to him, he generally learns it more effectively than do his students.

Therefore well-defined and recorded bodies of knowledge (i.e., "subjects") should be learned by the student in the process of teaching it to others. This does not apply to courses that involve learning a physical skill; for example, physical education, surveying, drafting, use of laboratory equipment, and speaking a foreign language. In these cases instruction by one who already has the skill is required.

But, given a number of students each of whom should learn a subject, each cannot teach it to all of the others. Therefore small groups of students (equal in size to the number of subjects required per semester; for example, five) should be organized into *learning cells* to share the responsibility of teaching each other the subjects being "taken." Each teaches the others one subject and is taught each of the other subjects by another in his cell.

Learning cells should be formed as follows. On registering each student would rank the subjects he intends to study in the order of teaching preference. Cells would be formed by combining students whose orderings over the same set of courses are as different as possible. All cells would work out teaching assignments and submit them to a faculty adviser who would mediate any conflicts. Cells could negotiate with each other for exchange of members but would have to settle their compositions with a specified period of time, say, one week.

The relevant faculty group will prepare a detailed specification of the *minimal* amount of the subject matter to be learned and will identify in an annotated bibliography the principal sources that can be used.

Each learning cell should be assigned to an office with desk and bookshelf space for each member.

Some questions that will arise in a student's mind in learning a subject will not be answered in the sources available to him, and the answers to others may be very difficult to find. Hence each learning cell should have a weekly tutorial. Graduate students would have approximately two hours with a member of the faculty for each subject being covered, and undergraduate students two hours with a graduate teaching assistant and one hour with a faculty member (with the teaching assistant present).

In addition each faculty member should have a regularly scheduled period of no less than three hours per week during which he is available to any student.

A standard examination should be given to all students to qualify them in a subject. A student obtains credit for a subject when he successfully completes the relevant examination.

A student may take an examination in a subject without having participated in a learning cell that covers the subject; that is, he may elect to teach it to himself.

Cheating is more an evil of the examination system than of the students. I say this because the typical closed-book examination is not an adequate model of any real situation in which a person must demonstrate his competence in a subject. Therefore examinations should be either open-book, take-home, or oral.

At least half of every examination should consist of answers to questions prepared by the student. He should formulate these questions in such a way as to best reveal what he believes to be his understanding of the subject. His questions, as well as his answers, should be evaluated.

In a subject which a student teaches to others he should receive not only his own grade in the examination but also the grades of those he has taught. The grades of the others should be weighted by their cumulative average grade in all subjects to cancel the effect of differences in ability.

To reduce the arbitrary nature of subjective grading or objectively gradable examinations only two grades should be used: Satisfactory and Unsatisfactory. But each faculty member who has responsibility for a student should prepare an appraisal of his ability and performance that will be entered in the student's file. A cumulative summary of his performance should be prepared annually by a faculty adviser who is assigned to the student throughout his degree program.

Enough of the example except to observe that this idealized concept, the learning cell, is being used or experimented with in at least six universities. The constraints that appear to make it infeasible seem to crumble once the idea is "bought." This is the point: planning should excite managers to the point where they strain sufficiently at the leash of tradition and custom to break with them. I know of no better way to bring them to such a point than to involve them in the idealized design process. (For further discussion of this process, see Nadler, 1967.)

SUMMARY

The means by which objectives and goals are pursued vary in generality, from the most particular (a course of action) through practices, procedures, and programs, to the most general (policies). Policies are decision rules that can incorporate all the relevant information available at the time of decision, and hence they can provide maximum flexibility and adaptability.

Planning is concerned not only with evaluating alternative means for attaining objectives but also with developing new and better ones. The key to both effective evaluation and design of alternatives lies in understanding the system being planned for. Understanding is most effectively captured in explanatory models of the system involved.

We are not yet capable of constructing usable models that represent all aspects of corporate systems nor even some of its major parts or functions. We can, however, model the parts and functions that are understood and link the models together so as to obtain at least partial representation of the system. Judgment and intuition must be used to supply the rest.

Modeling efforts should be directed at acquiring understanding of the firm, its supply system, its distribution and marketing system, its consumers, its competitors, and its environment. The better we understand these parts of the system and the relationships between them, the better can we evaluate available alternatives and create new ones.

Creation of new alternatives can often be facilitated by redesigning (from scratch) the system being planned for, with no constraints. Such an idealized conception of the system often reveals the desirability and feasibility of alternatives that would not otherwise have been considered. It tends to produce awareness and relaxation of self-imposed constraints and to elevate management's level of aspiration.

The policies yielded by the use of models are of two types: those involving operations of the existing system, and those involving changes in the system. The aspect of planning that is concerned with entering new businesses and the investments associated with such ventures has been treated more extensively in the literature than have most aspects (see, for example, Ansoff, 1965, and Hetrick, 1969).

Analysis and modeling of each of the six aspects of a business that have been considered reveal the possible courses of action and provide a basis for selecting among them. The most difficult part of policy planning, however, is bringing the policies and practices together into a cohesive whole. Such synthesis, as already observed, usually requires modification of the goals that were formulated earlier. In fact, if such reformulation is not made necessary by selection of policies and courses of action, the selection is subject to suspicion of being a mere rationalization of irrationally selected goals.

Now we turn to a consideration of the resources required to carry out the policies and courses of action that the planners have selected.

Chapter 4

RESOURCE PLANNING

INTRODUCTION

The resources required to operate a business can be placed into four classes:

1. Money.
2. Facilities and equipment.
3. Materials, supplies, and services.
4. Personnel (manpower).

In planning it is necessary to determine how much of each type of resource will be required by the courses of action and policies that have been selected. Therefore the first phase of resource planning requires determination of the amount and type of each resource that will be required for each year in the planning period.

Once these requirements have been estimated, it is necessary to determine how much of each type of resource can be expected to be available to the company at these times. Then, by comparing estimates of what will be available with estimates of what is required, one can determine how much of each type of resource one must plan to generate or acquire.

The second phase of resource planning should be devoted to determining whether the additional required resources can be generated or acquired, and how. If they can be made available when required, fine. If not, then it is necessary to modify previously established ends and means so as to reduce the resource requirements to a level that can be reached. It is also possible that such an analysis will reveal that more resources of one or more types will be available than will be required by the plan. In such a case it is necessary either to adjust previous planning decisions so as to use these resources effectively or to determine how the company can divest itself of them.

Finally the last phase of resource planning involves allocating the resources that are expected to be available to the programs and organizational units that will require them. Such an allocation is normally called budgeting, but budgeting is too often restricted to allocation of money. All four types of resources should be considered.

Currently available techniques and knowledge enable us to plan reasonably well for three of the four types of resource; personnel planning is the least developed. Hence I treat financial, facility, and material planning briefly but deal with personnel planning in some detail.

FINANCIAL PLANNING

Financial planning is the part of resource planning that is most familiar to most companies. In fact many companies mistakingly equate financial planning and corporate planning. Although it is important, it is only a small part of the total planning process.

Successful execution of financial planning requires the ability to forecast the financial position of the company for each year in the planning period and to do so under a wide variety of assumptions about policies and enviornmental conditions. A financial model of the firm is essential for this purpose. The accounting system of a company is such a model, but this system does not often lend itself to as rapid and easy manipulation as is required. Therefore an increasing number of companies have found it useful to computerize their financial model of the firm and thus have made it available as a tool in planning. The programming of the model can be designed so that its output is in a form that is familiar to, and well understood by, management.

A financial model can be used to predict what amounts of money will be available in specified years and how much of it will be required by the plans that have been formulated. Thus such a model makes it possible to determine what surplus or shortage of money can be expected if there is no planned intervention in its generation or acquisition.

If a future shortage is revealed and a decision is made to avoid it, a number of alternatives are available: a stock issue, borrowing from banks, sale and lease-back of facilities, and so on. These alternatives should be systematically evaluated so that an effective choice can be made. This type of decision has been extensively and intensively studied, and hence a great deal of guidance is available in the financial literature.

FACILITIES PLANNING

The theories and techniques of the management sciences that are relevant to the planning of facilities and equipment are very well developed. These include inventory theory, allocation theory, the techniques of mathematical programming, queuing theory, sequencing and coordination theory, the techniques of PERT and CPM, and replacement and maintenance theory. (See Ackoff and Rivett, 1963, Chapter 2, for a nontechnical discussion of these theories and techniques.) There are few aspects of facilities and equipment planning for which suitable modeling techniques and methods of solution are not available.

Once the requirements for additional facilities have been extracted from forecasts of future production requirements under the plan, the techniques of the management sciences can be applied quite rapidly to answering such questions as the following:

1. How large should the plant be? One may have a choice of building several small plants in different locations or one large plant. The relative advantages of these alternatives can be determined by use of available modeling techniques.

2. Where should a plant or plants be located? Given the locations of existing facilities and the forecast distribution of demand, it is possible to find the optimal location(s) of new facilities. These are usually locations that minimize the sum of a number of costs—including transportation in and out of the plant, land, labor, taxes, and so on.

3. Considering the uncertainties of demand and construction time, when should construction be initiated?

4. Once a plant is available, what production orders should be assigned to it so as to minimize the sum of the relevant production and transportation costs over the entire production system?

5. Which of alternative sources should be used to supply a new facility?

Not only can these and related questions be answered for proposed production facilities but the techniques that are useful in doing so are also applicable to similar questions concerning other types of facility, such as warehouses, retail stores, and even sales offices.

The techniques for handling questions raised in planning for equipment are also highly developed. Optimal decisions can be obtained for determining when equipment should be replaced either by new equipment of the same type or by technologically advanced models. It is also possible to develop optimal maintenance policies for plant and equipment. These of course are not independent of the replacement policy.

PLANNING MATERIALS AND SUPPLIES

The inputs required for the operation of a company may present no problem to planners. There may be no reason even to suspect that future supplies of raw material, utilities, and services will be deficient. But even where availability may be no problem, costs of these supplies may be subject to significant change. Possible increases in cost may be sufficiently large to justify a search for alternative materials or consideration of producing one's own raw materials. Planners should always consider the desirability of vertical integration on the input side of the business.

When a company accounts for a large share of the consumption of a raw material or components, its planning for the future obviously ought to involve consultation with its suppliers so that assurance of future supplies can be obtained.

PERSONNEL PLANNING

The term "manpower" is a heritage of the first industrial revolution, when men were thought of primarily as sources of physical power. For this reason, in my opinion, the term "personnel" is preferable; it better reflects contemporary concern with "the human use of human beings." But the use of the term "manpower planning" persists in both public and private planning.

The questions to which personnel planning is usually addressed are the following:

1. What is the minimal number of men by type that are required to meet the goals set in the plan?

2. What number of men by type should be recruited in each year of the planning period?

3. How should newly acquired personnel be allocated to organizational units?

Equally relevant problems that are less frequently considered because they involve the human (and hence sticky) aspects of human beings are the following:

4. How should personnel be recruited and selected so as to get employees that are as good as possible?

5. What type of education and training and how much of it should each type of personnel (new and old) receive in order (a) to maximize their ability to serve the organization now and in the future and (b) to satisfy their own needs and desires? More generally, how should careers in the organization be designed and programmed?

6. How should tasks be designed so that both maximum productivity and satisfaction are yielded by them?

7. How can the work environment (physical, economic, and social) be developed so that each individual is motivated both to work as closely as possible to the limits of his capabilities and to extend his capabilities?

Unlike the last four questions, the first three (personnel numbers) deal with people in a way that does not directly involve their human characteristics. Let us consider these three questions first.

Number of People Required

An answer to the question, "What is the minimal number of men by type that are required to meet the various goals set in planning?", should be sought bearing in mind that the level of recruiting of (particularly professional) personnel cannot be reduced drastically from one year to the next without adversely affecting recruiting efforts in succeeding years.

Organizational goals are frequently set before personnel-planning requirements are finally determined, and hence these requirements are not taken into account in formulating the goals. In principle one would like to set organizational goals in such a way that some function of gain and loss (e.g., profit) is maximized. Most personnel-planning procedures in current use provide no assurance that any function of income and cost is maximized. To obtain such maximization, however, it is necessary (but not sufficient) to minimize personnel requirements for any level of income at which goals are set.

If organizational goals are set independently of personnel requirements, it seems natural to attempt to minimize the number of men required. This is equivalent to maximizing the productivity of men. However, it is only equivalent to minimizing the *cost* of personnel when the cost per man is independent of type. This is seldom the case because different types of personnel are usually compensated differently. If goals are set before establishing personnel requirements, and various types of personnel are involved, planning should minimize the *cost* of personnel, not the number of men.

The Personnel Response Function

Where a relatively large number of people are involved in the same kind of task it is necessary to employ (explicitly or implicitly) a *personnel response function* if one wants to minimize either the number or cost of personnel. Such a function relates the amount of personnel allocated to a specific activity to the amount of return realized from that activity. Such response functions usually take the shape shown in Figure 4.1, in which marketing personnel is used as an illustration.

A certain amount of marketing effort is required before an account begins to respond; for example, a call by one salesman once a year may not be likely to yield any sales. The point at which the response "takes off" is called the *threshold*. In general the response then increases approximately in proportion to the amount of effort until the customer responds as much as he can or is willing to. At this point the customer is "saturated." Additional sales effort beyond this point generally has little positive effect. At the "supersaturation point" the account begins to respond negatively because the sales effort becomes offensive.

If one had such a curve for each of a specified set of actual and potential accounts, it would be possible and quite simple to use

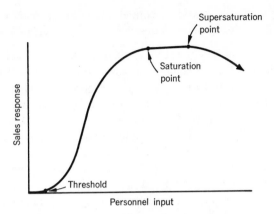

FIGURE 4.1 Typical form of a personnel response function.

available techniques to determine the amount of personnel that would maximize profit or some other function of income and expense.

If one must settle for less than a personnel response function for each activity, and one usually has to, one would like to find such a function for classes of activities with similar response functions. The response function of a class of activities would represent the average response one would get from activities applied to the class for each amount of personnel input. Use of such *aggregated* response functions results in less accurate but usually adequate approximations for maximization of profit or minimization of personnel requirements.

Scientifically based personnel planning must use one of the two types of response function. Without an explicit response function planning is essentially judgmental, no matter how quantitative the analyses that are involved. Because of the amount of experimentation (and hence time and cost) that their development requires, most personnel planners do not have, and do not try to develop, personnel response functions.

The use of implicit response functions (i.e., ones "in the planner's head") provides no way of checking their consistency and accuracy, and hence there is no systematic way of improving them.

Manpower planners commonly use a linear response function that is obtained by fitting a straight line to a set of points representing jointly observed personnel inputs and associated outputs. Such a procedure suffers from several serious deficiencies.

1. Even if the "correct" line were obtained by sheer luck, it would fit the true personnel response function only between the threshold and saturation point (see Figure 4.1). Hence it would incorrectly predict possible increases in response where none or negative responses would in fact occur.

2. Even if a line with a significant slope were obtained for a class of activities, it does not follow that the property defining the class of activities (e.g., size or type of account) is *causally* related to performance. For example, if we plot gross annual sales obtained by companies in a given industry against their annual advertising expenditures, a line with a significant slope can be found. This does not mean that increased advertising produces increased sales. What it does mean is that most companies in an industry set their advertising budgets at approximately the same percentage of their forecast sales. The line thus shows how forecasts of sales cause advertising, not how advertising causes sales. (Advertising response functions have the same shape as personnel response functions.) Similarly it is not unlikely that a forecast of sales to an account has more effect on the amount of personnel allocated to the account than the amount of personnel allocated has on the sales to the account.

The fact that different industries have different advertising response lines does not mean that "type of industry" is relevant to the effect of advertising on sales. It does mean that the type of industry is relevant to the effect of forecasts of sales on advertising expenditures. Similarly it is not unlikely that "type of customer" influences the amount of marketing personnel allocated to it more that the amount of personnel allocated to it influences the amount sold. In short, the fitting of straight lines to historical data by statistical or other techniques cannot by itself uncover causal relations between levels of personnel input and the associated outputs.

3. In general currently used planning procedures try to extract an *explanation* of personnel productivity from a *description* of past performance. These procedures are based on the hope that, if historical data are properly classified and analyzed, a satisfactory

explanation will emerge. This is a vain hope. Theories and explanations are not successfully developed by classifications. To be sure, past behavior may *suggest* an explanation, but construction of a theory is more an act of reflection and imagination than it is of data analysis. Theories can be tested by using data from the past, present, and future—and progressively improved as a result. However, the data used to test a theory should not be the same as those that suggested it. A relationship between variables that is obtained by fitting a line to relevant data cannot be tested for its predictive or explanatory power on the same data from which it was derived. Yet efforts to do just this are common to many personnel-planning procedures. Without some experimentation it is very unlikely that a company will ever develop a sound basis for planning.

4. The use of lines fitted to past data in personnel planning can *at best* ensure only continuation of previously attained levels of efficiency. Furthermore it can only do this much if the activity and the involved system do not change significantly. Most of these activities and systems do change in significant ways over time, often because of technological changes in the involved processes.

5. If lines are fitted to different classes of activity to relate their outputs to personnel inputs, the classification scheme that is used is critical. The classes should contain activities whose outputs are very much alike, and each class should have a fundamentally different response function. A number of statistical techniques for forming such classes have been developed, but they are not commonly used as yet.

Too much effort has been wasted trying to find easy ways of estimating future personnel requirements. The understanding that is required for the development of effective estimating procedures requires more research than is usually associated with personnel planning. There follows a relatively detailed example of how research has been used fruitfully in the personnel-planning process.

An Example of Research on Personnel Requirements

Although complete knowledge of relevant personnel response functions is necessary for completely effective manpower planning, partial knowledge can nevertheless yield results of considerable value. Consider, for example, a study conducted in association with a long-range planning effort of General Electric's Lamp Division (for a detailed account of this work see Waid, Clark, and Ackoff, 1956).

As part of the planning process it was necessary to determine how many additional salesmen would be required in each of the next five years. These estimates were originally prepared by assuming that the average number of accounts covered by salesmen at the time was optimal. The planners did not have time to investigate this assumption. As a result the plan that was produced (see Glover and Ackoff, 1956) specified a large number of additional salesmen in each of the next five years.

The planners felt sufficiently insecure about this requirement to recommend that an operations-research project be initiated to determine the average number of accounts that should be assigned to salesmen. The recommendation was accepted. The following is a brief account of the project that resulted.

An analysis of call reports prepared by salesmen revealed that that change in the number of sales calls made on accounts in two successive years had no relationship to changes in the amounts sold to these accounts or to the percentage changes in these amounts. This result was found to hold for every class of account no matter how complex or sophisticated a classification scheme was used.

In order to check carefully this surprising result another type of analysis was carried out. Accounts were classified by whether they had had an increase or decrease in the number of sales calls in 1953 as compared with 1952. They were then subclassified according to whether or not the number of sales calls made on them in 1954 was an increase or decrease over 1953. This yielded four classes of account:

	Changes in Number of Calls	
Class	1952–1953	1953–1954
1	Increase	Increase
2	Increase	Decrease
3	Decrease	Increase
4	Decrease	Decrease

No significant differences were found in the average changes in amounts sold to accounts in these classes.

Both analyses showed that on the average the number of sales calls being made on accounts fell on the plateau between the saturation and supersaturation points of the sales response function.

How could these results be used for personnel-planning purposes? They suggested that some reduction in number of calls (and therefore in number of salesmen) could be made without reducing sales. But how much of a reduction? The maximum reduction that could be justified by available data would result from cutting back each account to the smallest number of calls per year that it had received over the three-year period studied. If, for example, an account had received 60 calls in 1952, 40 in 1953, and 50 in 1954, the number of future annual calls could be reduced to 40. In the absence of detailed knowledge of the underlying sales response functions this was a conservative conclusion. Larger reductions could probably have been made for many accounts, but the available data could not justify them.

This last analysis revealed that a 20 percent reduction in sales calls could be expected to have no effect on sales volume. However it raised the question as to whether assigning more accounts to salesmen—in order to obtain the reduced number of calls per account and to reduce the sales force—would affect the average return from individual sales calls. An analysis was made of the performance of those salesmen in one district who already carried more accounts than were recommended by the researchers. It revealed that these salesmen had a higher average return per call than the other salesmen in their district and that they had obtained a higher total amount of sales.

The data collected for the preceding studies made some additional analyses possible. In one sales district a time study of salesmen had been carried out. In addition to their regular call report they had provided specially requested information on each call they had made during a particular month. They had recorded the mileage, travel time, waiting time, and interview time associated with each call. They had also recorded the amount of administrative time spent in their offices or at home.

This supplementary data covered only 9 of over 300 salesmen, and only for one month. Therefore, no general conclusions could be drawn. Nevertheless some of the results were consistent enough over the sample to indicate that they probably held generally. Some of the more important of these results were as follows:

1. Travel time was related to distance traveled only within wide limits. A more important factor was apparently the kind of territory. Calls in metropolitan areas consumed much more travel time than might be expected; those in rural areas, much less than expected. The travel time per call in the sample was almost identical for urban and rural territories, although the average distance traveled per call was twice as great in the rural areas. The most stable estimate of travel time turned out to be a percentage of total time and therefore to be independent of the distance traveled.

2. Waiting time was an insignificant portion of total time. It was about six minutes on the average and the same regardless of the type of account involved. It was not related to the size of account, as had been expected.

3. Interview time varied for different types of account, but it did not differ for the four major classes of accounts.

4. Administrative time was a higher proportion of total time than had been expected.

It was possible to estimate the "dollars sold per sales call" for each type of account. This was equivalent to estimating the cost of sales by type of account, information that had not previously been available to management. By use of the cost information it was possible to estimate the amount of profit derived from each class of account. This in turn provided an estimate of net return per sales dollar spent on each type of account. Differences in this return were as great as eight to one among major classes of account, and several hundred to one among minor classes. These results indicated that the practice of allocating sales costs proportionately to sales volume leads to serious errors. The appropriate accounting changes were made.

The analysis was extended to include calls on prospects that were converted into accounts. These "realized" prospects were classified in the same way as accounts, and return per call was determined for both the sum of "before conversion" and "after conversion" calls per year, and for "after conversion" calls alone. It was found that on the average new accounts yielded considerably less return per call (in the first year) than did old accounts. Certain classes of new accounts, however, yielded more return per call in their first year than did certain other classes of old accounts.

This indicated that a reallocation of calls, reducing the number on certain types of old account and increasing the number on certain types of prospects, would increase the productivity of sales calls.

Finally an analysis was carried out to determine how many unsuccessful calls should be made on a prospect before abandoning him. A table was prepared listing the number of prospects and the number of calls made on them over the two-year period 1952–1953. A similar compilation with modified data is shown in Table 4.1. In the actual data as many as 40 calls had been made on a prospect in one year.

An analysis of the modified data given in Table 4.1 shows that a maximum of three calls per prospect yields the maximum return in average numbers of accounts obtained per cell. If this policy had been followed, assuming that additional prospects of the same type could have been found (a safe assumption in this case), 248 calls (1148 − 900) would have been made on these prospects. This number of calls would yield an expected 18 (248/13.8) accounts. The data in the table indicate that these calls "actually" produced only eight (73 − 65) new accounts. Thus the policy of a maximum of three calls per prospect could yield a 14 percent increase in the number of new accounts (from 73 to 83) with the same number of calls. In the real case an increase of 11 percent was indicated.

TABLE 4.1 Prospect-Call Analysis

Number of Calls	Cumulative Number of Accounts Obtained	Cumulative Number of Prospects Dropped	Cumulative Totals, Number of Calls	Number of Calls per Conversion
1	30	220	500	16.7
2	50	300	750	15.0
3	65	325	900	13.8
4	70	350	1010	14.4
5	72	370	1090	15.1
6	73	380	1148	15.7

On the basis of these analyses several actions were taken, the most important of which in this context was that planned additions to the sales force were curtailed. Planned sales goals were nevertheless met. The annual saving obtained by *not* acquiring the additional salesmen originally recommended was approximately twenty-five times the cost of these studies.

Some Problems in Personnel-Numbers Planning

The personnel-numbers planning procedures that have been discussed are applicable wherever relatively large numbers of people are involved in essentially the same type of task. In most companies, however, there are usually a large number of tasks in each of which relatively few are engaged but which collectively involve many people. Furthermore, even where numbers are involved in similar tasks, the structure or environment of these tasks may change so rapidly as to preclude derivation of relevant response functions from history. If such functions are obtained, their applicability is at best short lived; for example, if the involved personnel are salesmen and their product is subject to rapid and significant technological change (as has been the case in computers), responsiveness to selling effort for one technology may have little relevance to such effort for another technology. Furthermore, as the mix of initial, replacement, and expansion sales change, so may the response function.

Centralized personnel planning is likely to be very difficult or even ineffective in such situations. Even where centralized personnel planning is possible, the adaptive planner is likely to try to place responsibility for acquiring men on the units that will use them and to develop measures of the performance of such units that will motivate their managers to seek optimal personnel levels. He would also provide research assistance to these managers so that they can better estimate their requirements and evaluate their previous estimates. Then estimates of unit personnel requirements would be fed to the corporate planning group. This group may have to modify these estimates in order to take into account planned changes in corporate directions with which low-level organizational units may not be familiar. Nevertheless such adjustments in their estimates should be discussed with lower level units so that they understand the rationale behind the changes.

The principal objection to such a decentralized personnel-planning procedure lies in the requirement for making small units conscious of costs as well as income. It is argued correctly that this can put undue emphasis on short-run profits and deemphasize longer run development. This problem of course is not specific to personnel planning but arises whenever a "profit center" is created. What is required is a measure of performance that reflects not only what has actually transpired in the period evaluated but also a change in future potential. This need is even more relevant at the corporate level, as my earlier discussion of profit(ability) indicated. Therefore, whatever the solution to this problem that is found at the corporate level, it can also be applied at the unit level of the organization.

Coming back to the situation in which small numbers are involved in each of a large number of different tasks, each cannot be planned for separately. Such tasks must be planned for in the aggregate, seeking as much flexibility in the involved personnel as is possible. There is no better protection against the cost of errors in personnel planning than having personnel who can be moved from one type of task to another and who are proficient—or capable of becoming so—in a wide variety of tasks.

Minority Personnel Planning

Minority Personnel Planning is becoming more prevalent because of both increased pressure from federal and state governments, and an increased social conscience. A relatively obvious logic for such planning involves the following steps in one variation or another:

1. The percentage of minority-group members who work in the company is compared with the percentage in the labor market from which employees are drawn. There is usually a gap to be closed, and such closing is formulated as an objective that is often identified as a "fair share" or "proportional representation" objective.

2. The percentage of minority workers in each unit and category of personnel in the company is determined, and this is compared with the overall company percentage. The objective here is usually to approach the same percentage in each unit and category as the company has as a whole. This is sometimes called a balance objective.

3. The minority labor market is surveyed for the skills available

in it, and in light of the findings feasible "share" and "balance" goals (usually annual) are set.

4. Alternative training programs are evaluated with respect to their ability to reduce the difference between what is estimated to be a *feasible* share and balance and a *fair* share and balance. A selection is made from such programs on the basis of some kind of cost-effectiveness evaluation.

5. Consideration is sometimes given to the problem of integrating minority workers into the organization. To assist in doing so programs are sometimes designed to make majority workers more tolerant of minority workers.

Such planning represents a considerable advance over the kind of indifference or antagonism to minorities that helped produce the current racial crisis in the United States. But the sense of righteousness that often accompanies such efforts should not obscure their shortcomings.

First note that, unless *every* employer seeks to employ a "fair share" of the minority group, equal employment for its members cannot be obtained. Not every company does, nor is every company likely to do so. Furthermore, since a "fair share" is set as a target (and hence is a *maximum* share to be obtained), undershooting is more likely to occur than overshooting. This also reduces the chances of equal minority employment. Therefore, if a company is unwilling to hire more than its "fair share," it must be prepared either to support governmental programs that will care for those not taken care of by private enterprise or, if the government does not do so, to suffer the effects of the turbulent society that will be a consequence of failing to do so.

Second, such programs as are usually conceived and considered in this type of planning are not likely to be effective relative to the "hard core" of the unemployed. Members of this "core" are usually so alienated from the culture of the majority, and hence so uncomfortable in or repelled by it, that they either will not accept work out of their neighborhoods or, if they do, will not stick with it. Thus there is a great need for increased employment opportunities in the neighborhoods in which they reside, employment that can provide a transition so that more will be willing in time to work outside their neighborhoods. For this reason minority personnel planning should consider establishing company-owned or company-operated establishments in the ghetto that will employ significant numbers of otherwise unemployable persons. In designing such operations it is necessary to relax the notion of training men to fit a job, at least initially, and to use ingenuity in designing jobs to fit the men and to motivate them to seek new skills and advancement.

Indigenous self-development groups in the ghetto should be invited to participate in the design and operation of such programs. Not only can they contribute conceptually but they can also apply effective pressure to keep men on their jobs in their neighborhood. Furthermore such involvement by indigenous groups strengthens them and thus further accelerates development in the ghetto.

In some areas it may be difficult for some companies to launch such programs on their own. Therefore collaboration with other companies may be necessary. Assistance from local universities and colleges should also be sought.

To engage successfully in this broader concept of minority personnel planning a senior manager should be involved in it, and such involvement should be his major responsibility. This manager should be an "up and comer," not a "down and goner" who is put out in the minority pasture. The latter practice, which unfortunately is quite common, often evokes justifiable minority labeling of company efforts as "tokenism."

The Human Use of Human Beings

Now let us consider questions 4 to 7, which involve design of recruiting and selection procedures (4), educational, training, and career-development programs (5), tasks and jobs (6), and the total work environment (7). Answering these questions clearly should involve a deep understanding of human nature and hence can be illuminated by the relevant types of behavioral science. (I have found the type of approach taken by F. E. Emery and Eric L. Trist, 1969, to be particularly useful.)

Why should such specific personnel problems be of concern to the corporate planner rather than to the personnel department? The human being (even the manager) is a special kind of resource because he is capable of making choices. Therefore he must be motivated properly if he is to perform properly. Without such motivation the best laid plans of men often go astray. Certainly a responsive organization must consist of people whose individual objectives are well served when those of the organization are.

Human beings cannot be programmed like equipment. The more people are treated like equipment, the more do they behave like it; that is, they deteriorate with use, require frequent repair, break down, and become technologically obsolete. All this can be avoided.

Although human beings are, in a sense, general-purpose computers, they cannot perform all functions equally well. Therefore we cannot design tasks or careers for them without taking into account their unique capabilities and propensities. Structure must be fitted to people because people cannot always be fitted to structure. The current upheaval in nations, cities, and universities over participative democracy is striking evidence of this point. Therefore planners should be concerned with both the fit of people to the organization and the fit of the organization to its people.

It is as fruitless to "explain" uncooperative or inefficient behavior of employees by attributing irrationality to them, as it is to do so to consumers. (See the earlier discussion of the latter on page 51.) Close examination reveals that much (if not most) apparently irrational behavior of employees is rational behavior in an irrational environment created by the organization. Consider the following brief examples.

Executives of one corporation complained because their district managers "always asked for authorization for more salesmen than they needed." Inquiry revealed that these managers were compensated through an incentive system that credited them for the amount sold in their districts but did not debit them for the cost of selling. Furthermore, since experience had taught the district managers that their personnel requests were always cut back in an arbitrary manner, they deliberately overestimated their needs in hope of getting the number that they really wanted. There was nothing irrational in their behavior, but there was in the incentive system applied to them and in the way their requests for personnel were processed.

Another company had a very large number of repairmen on the streets in company trucks in which they carried a supply of replacement parts. Because of the large number of repairmen, the total truck-borne parts inventory was huge. Company executives point out that on any one day a repairman only "did a few jobs but nevertheless loaded his truck to the roof with parts." It turned out that the repairmen were on an incentive system that was based on the number of repairs completed per day and took no account of the amount of stock they tied up. A return to the warehouse during the day to pick up a part reduced their earnings.

Production planners in another company complained about the poor quality of sales forecasts supplied to them by the marketing department. But they were forbidden communication with the forecasters in the marketing department because the production and marketing vice presidents were not on speaking terms. Therefore the production planners ignored the forecasts that were sent to them and developed their own, which are better. When asked why their forecasts were so poor, the sales forecasters in the marketing department replied, "Why improve them? Production doesn't use them anyhow." The irrationality was in the bifurcated environment, not in the behavior of the nonmanagerial personnel involved.

Experimentation on Personnel Problems

When dealing with something as poorly understood as the productivity of people, it is almost always necessary to use controlled experiments to test and improve explanations and predictions of their behavior. Such experiments, if properly designed, can be small in scale and need not significantly disrupt normal operations. These experiments should not require any more changes, or changes of larger magnitude, in personnel allocations than are often made in normal operations.

In one case, for example, it was possible to select at random 27 market areas out of 198 and to divide them into three groups of nine each. One group had its field selling force reduced by 25 percent, the second had no change, and the third was given a 25 percent increase. By analyzing differences between actual and forecast sales in these areas, it was possible within six months to determine the effect on sales of these levels of effort. Doing so was sufficient to improve personnel allocations without optimizing them. Continued exeprimentation on a relatively small scale permitted the response function to be reasonably estimated within two years.

It is possible to experiment with every aspect of personnel management, even the most qualitative. The power of such experimentation is reflected in a report of *The Observer*, May 9, 1969, selections from which follow:

"Five years of experiments in Holland are paying off. N. U. Philips' Gloeilampenfabrieken, the giant radio and pharmaceuticals firm, has invented 'work structuring'—described as a revolution in thinking about production, people and profits."

"The documented results from 30 major investigations are irresistible."

"Research by the company's department of industrial psychology revealed that of the people who left the firm, 94 percent considered the job security to be good and payment adequate, 57 percent thought the management was satisfactory, but only 37 percent liked the work itself."

"Instead of making people change to suit the firm's need, the reverse is happening."

"Work is being arranged so that it fits the motivations and capacities of the people available."

"Substantial savings in labour have resulted. The use of 'indirect' manpower, for example, has been cut by 30 percent in four years."

It will be a long time before firms can survey their workers and find, as Philips did after a restructuring exercise, that 91 percent replied: 'I like my job.' "

Recognition of the need for, and the nature of, responsive personnel experiments is a responsibility of corporate planners. No other group in a corporation can better perceive systematic individual-organization mismatches and ways of correcting them.

SUMMARY

Resource planning should cover (a) determination of requirements for, (b) plans for acquisition or generation of, and (c) allocation of four types of resources: money; facilities and equipment; materials, supplies, and services; and personnel.

Financial planning procedures are generally well developed in most companies. Essential to this process is a financial model of the firm, preferably computerized, into which different plans can be "inserted" and which will then yield a picture of the company's finances under the plan for each year in the planning period.

Facilities planning can be greatly aided by use of the theories and techniques of the management sciences. These enable one to determine optimally (or approximately so) the size of future facilities, their location, the time they should be available, the assignment of work to them, and how to supply them. Equipment can be similarly treated, and relevant replacement and maintenance policies can also be developed by the use of available procedures.

Materials and supplies for the future should be checked to determine whether they will be available in sufficient amounts and at acceptable costs. If not, the possibility of vertical integration and self-supply should be considered.

Personnel planning is in general the least developed aspect of resource planning. It is usually carried out on a piecemeal basis using extrapolations from past performance for estimating future requirements. Such procedures can at best only assure continuation of previously attained levels of efficiency. Effective personnel planning requires developing personnel response functions that show the causal connection between number and type of personnel assigned to a task and output. Development of such functions usually requires some experimentation, much of which can be done without serious disruption of normal operations. Even with partial information and understanding that can be obtained in this way significant improvements in the use of personnel can often be realized.

Effective use of personnel can sometimes result from application of appropriately designed incentives systems for those who use such personnel. Planning can then be based on their personnel-requirements estimates, modifying them where necessary to fit higher level plans.

Minority personnel planning is receiving increasing attention. The search for a "fair share" and "balance" of minority employees, as they are usually defined, is not likely to yield a solution to our related social problems. Creating employment within urban ghettos is a necessary condition to obtaining such a solution.

Corporate planners should be concerned with the human use of human beings because these free-willed individuals can either destroy a plan or magnify its benefits. Which they do depends on how well their own and the organization's objectives are coordinated. In attempting to understand and explain the behavior of employees it is usually more fruitful to attribute rationality to them and seek an explanation for their "undesirable" behavior in the irrationality of their oganizational environment than vice versa.

When as little understanding and precise knowledge exist as in the personnel area, experimentation is an almost indispensible instrument of planning for it.

Personnel and organizational planning cannot be conducted separately. Their separation, even for purposes of discussion, is forced. Therefore we turn immediately to the subject of organizational planning.

Chapter 5

ORGANIZATIONAL DESIGN

INTRODUCTION

A plan has little value if the organization planned for is not capable of carrying it out. Hence a plan may require reorganization of the system involved or it may stimulate reorganization that is required independently of the plan. Taking the organization's structure for granted may deprive the planner of his most powerful means of improving its performance.

As mentioned in Chapter 1, satisficing planners try to leave organizational structure alone because proposals for structural changes tend to breed opposition. Optimizing planners are inclined to avoid organizational considerations except where they obstruct optimization of operations. In general optimizers do not look at organizational structure as something to be optimized, but they can be expected to do so when the required mathematical techniques, which are now under development, are ready for such use. (Some of these techniques are discussed subsequently in this chapter; for discussion of some others see Cooper, Leavitt, and Shelly, 1964, particularly Part 4.) The adaptive planner, however, sees changes of organizational structure as one of his most effective means of improving system performance. He believes that, if he designs an organization that is foresightful, innovative, and rational, much of the need for planning is removed. For such an organization there will be fewer and less intense problems, and opportunities are more likely to be seen and effectively exploited.

Organizational planning should be directed toward the following objectives:

1. To identify physical and mental tasks that need to be done.
2. To group tasks into jobs that can be done well and to assign

87

responsibility for doing them to some individual or group; that is, to arrange functions and responsibilities.

3. To provide workers at all levels (a) with the information and other resources necessary for doing their jobs as effectively as possible, including feedback on their actual performance; (b) with measures of performance that are compatible with organizational objectives and goals; and (c) with motivation for performing as well as they can.

In comprehensive planning every member of the organization should be covered by the steps listed. Planning at the corporate level, however, is only a part of comprehensive planning; planning is also required at every other level of the organization. The goals and policies specified at the corporate level should direct the attention of lower level planners to the three objectives of organizational planning and provide guidance in the selection of relevant goals and policies. In planning at the corporate level the structure of management should be considered in detail. It is this aspect of organizational structure with which we are primarily concerned in this discussion.

Planning for the three organizational objectives listed above can be accomplished by the following steps, each of which is considered in more detail below:

1. Decision-flow analysis: identification of decisions that should be made by managers.

2. Modeling each managerial decision where possible, no matter how crudely.

3. Determination of the information required by each decision and design of a management information system that will fill these requirements.

4. Design of jobs: grouping decisions into job descriptions, assigning responsibility for them, identifying those decisions that are to be made by groups, and specifying the organization of group decision making.

5. Development of (a) measures of performance; (b) procedures for making the measurements, and disseminating and using the results; and (c) incentive systems for motivating personnel to perform as well as they can.

DECISION-FLOW ANALYSIS

Decision making is an essential activity of managers. Yet in discussing organizational design we usually make explicit how managers are related to each other, but not how the decisions that they make are or should be related. Analysis and synthesis of organizational structure should begin with analysis and synthesis of decisions.

The objective of decision-flow analysis is to identify the managerial decisions that are required to operate the business and the relationships between them. The output can usually best be represented by a diagram that looks much like one prepared as a basis for programming a computer to do the tasks.

The best way to start this job is to develop an accurate and detailed description of how the system actually operates. This can proceed in the following way:

1. *Determine whose needs or desires, external to the organization, the organization tries to satisfy.* This involves identifying the consumers and the type of goods or services that they want and that the company can provide.

2. *Determine how this need or desire is communicated to the organization;* for example, the need may be communicated in the form of an order given to a salesman.

3. *Determine how the needed information is recorded and transmitted to others in the organization.*

The last point may be illustrated by the following example. An order or requisition is usually prepared in multiple copies. Each of these copies should be followed to its ultimate disposition: destruction or permanent file. At each point at which the information is received a determination should be made of what happens to it. In general two kinds of things can happen to it.

First, the information can be transformed in several ways. It may be translated into coded form, condensed, expanded, consolidated, and so on. The result is usually the preparation of a new form, which also is prepared in multiple copies. These should be traced to their ultimate destinations, and so on.

Second, at some points in the system the information may be

used to reach a decision and to issue instructions. From such points instructions should be followed to their consummation. In most systems one form of instruction results in the ordering and eventual receipt of resources in the system (e.g., raw material or money). The flow of resources should then be followed through its processing. Instructions emanating from the flow of information will meet resource processing at key points, which should be noted. Ultimately the finished product or service is delivered to the customer. This in turn usually initiates a flow of money and information relevant to it.

Once this information has been collected, it can be subjected to the following type of analysis. First, all transmissions of information that do not produce a decision or action—so-called information copies—can be ignored. Operations on resources that occur between control points can be combined into one composite operation.

Figure 5.1 shows a typical initial recording of information. Figure 5.2 is a diagram of the production activities of a machine-tool company's operations, prepared after the initial information had been analyzed. With such a diagram one can begin to determine what types of decisions are required for performing the functions indicated by boxes in the diagram; for example, it is apparent that in Purchasing, decisions must be made as to the supplier to be used, the amount to be ordered, and perhaps the way the goods should be shipped.

Such analysis can reveal points at which control can be, but is not being, exercised. For example, in the process represented in Figure 5.2 it was found that parts were classified into those to be made by the company and those to be bought from others. This was done on the basis of analyses made at the time the part was designed. These decisions had never been reviewed since, although some of the parts had been in production for two decades or more. A systematic and frequent review of all make-or-buy decisions was subsequently installed.

Even if one begins with an analysis of only part of the business, he can push the analysis back until he reaches higher level and more strategic decisions. For example, the fact that a machine was sold presupposes a decision to offer it for sale. This can only be done after it has been developed. A decision had to be made to invest in its development and an amount to be invested had to be determined.

By combining the descriptive and analytical processes outlined here it is possible to identify the decisions required to run the business and to show their interdependence in diagrammatic form. The planners are not likely to have the time to do all the required work. Access to systems analysts is therefore essential.

Once such an analysis has been made, it need not be redone each time a plan is prepared or revised, it need only be kept up to date.

MODEL CONSTRUCTION

I have already discussed the nature and use of models in planning, but here I take up the use of models in a particular context,

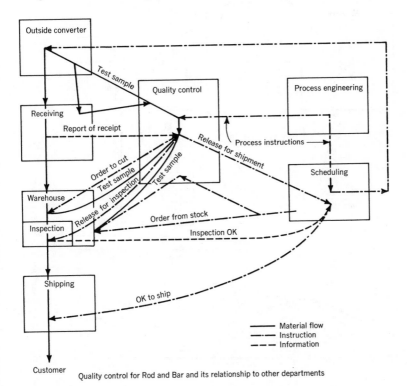

Quality control for Rod and Bar and its relationship to other departments

FIGURE 5.1 Example of initial notes in a system analysis.

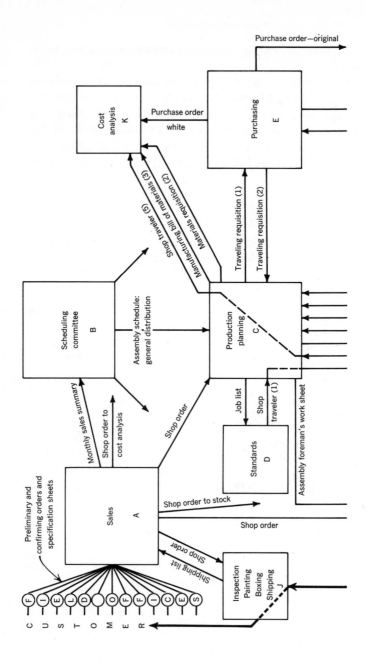

FIGURE 5.2 Control and materials flow chart.

92

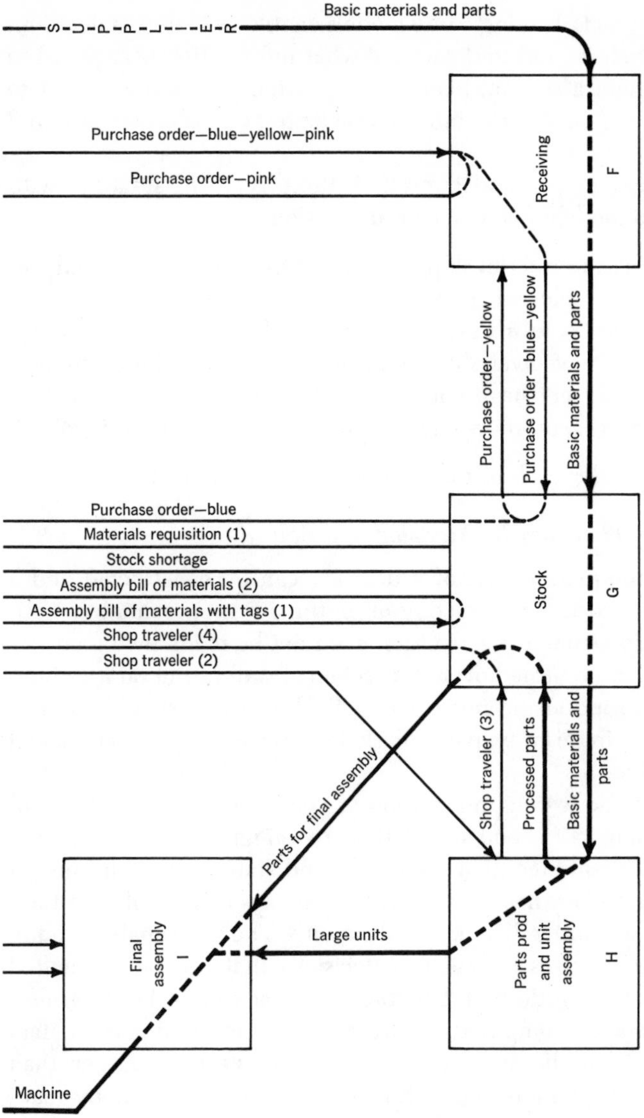

Basic materials and parts

S-U-P-P-L-I-E-R

Purchase order—blue—yellow—pink

Purchase order—pink

Receiving   F

Purchase order—yellow

Purchase order—blue—yellow

Basic materials and parts

Purchase order—blue
Materials requisition (1)
Stock shortage
Assembly bill of materials (2)
Assembly bill of materials with tags (1)
Shop traveler (4)
Shop traveler (2)

Stock   G

Shop traveler (3)

Processed parts

Basic materials and parts

Parts for final assembly

Final assembly   I

Large units

Parts prod and unit assembly   H

Machine

93

FIGURE 5.2.

organizational planning. Here models enable us to design decision-making systems and to determine what information is required to support such a system; hence they provide an essential input to the design of managerial information systems, a subject considered in Chapter 6.

The planner can find himself in three types of situation with respect to modeling a managerial decision:

1. He has, or can develop, a model of the decision involved and can extract a solution from it.

2. He has, or can develop, a model of the decision involved but does not have available a way of extracting a solution from it.

3. He does not have and cannot develop (because of lack of time, resources, or knowledge) a model of the decision involved.

Let us consider each of these situations in more detail.

Decisions That Can Be Modeled and Solved

If an adequate model of a decision can be constructed and a procedure exists for extracting an optimal or approximately optimal solution from it, the decision need not be made by a manager at all; it can be turned over to a technical staff or put on a computer. Many routine and repetitive tactical decisions should and can be handled in this way, particularly in purchasing, production, and distribution.

An obstacle to computerization of decisions is the reluctance of some managers to cede any of their sovereignty to the computer. They mistakenly feel that their tasks and status are diminished in the process. They need not. There are always more problems for a manager to handle than he can deal with. The less capable tend to involve themselves so much in decisions that can be automated that they have little time left for those that cannot be. Decisions that cannot be computerized are generally more important than those that can be since they tend to be strategic rather than tactical. Furthermore the computer must be controlled by managers. This is a new and important managerial task created by automatic decision making. Failure to take responsibility for a computer system that does part of a manager's job, by that manager, can have serious consequences.

Let me cite a case in point. The chairman of the board of an equipment manufacturing company asked for help on the following problem. One of his larger (decentralized) divisions had installed a computerized production-inventory control system about a year earlier. The system involved about $2,000,000 worth of equipment. The chairman had just received a request from the division for permission to replace the original equipment with new equipment that was several times more costly than the first installation. An extensive "justification" for the expenditure was provided with the request. The chairman wanted to know whether the request was really justified. He admitted to complete ignorance in this area.

A meeting was arranged at the division's headquarters during which I was given an extended and detailed briefing. The system was large but relatively simple. At the heart of it was a reorder point for each item and a maximum allowable stock level. Reorder points took demand and lead time into account. The computer kept track of stock, ordered items when required, and generated numerous reports on both the state of the system and its own behavior.

When the briefing was over, I was asked if I had any questions. I did. First I asked whether, when the system had been installed, there had been many parts whose stock level exceeded the maximum allowable amount under the new controls. I was told that there had been many. I asked for a list of about thirty and for some graph paper. Both were provided. With the help of the system coordinator and many old reports I began to plot the stock level over time of the first item on the list. When this item had come down to the maximum allowable stock level for the first time, much to the surprise of those in attendance, it had been reordered. Continued plotting showed that the item had been reordered every time it approached this maximum level. Clearly the computer program was confusing the maximum allowable stock level and the reorder point. This turned out to be the case for more than half the items on my list.

Next I asked if they had many paired parts, ones that were used only with each other; for example, matched nuts and bolts. They had many. A list was produced and I began to check the recorded withdrawals for the previous day. For many of the pairs the differences in the numbers recorded as withdrawn were very large. No explanation could be provided.

On the basis of these and other questions and some "quick and

dirty" calculations it was possible to show that the new computerized system was costing the company almost $150,000 per month
more than the hand-operated system it had replaced, exclusive of
the cost of equipment. The cost was for excessive inventories.

I recommended that the system be redesigned as quickly as
possible and that the new equipment not be authorized for the
time being.

The questions that I had asked were obvious and simple ones.
Managers should have asked them—and this is the point—they
felt incompetent to do so. They would not have allowed a hand-
operated system to get so far out of control. Managers have the
same responsibility for control of computerized systems as they
have for ones that are hand operated.

Controlling a computerized system can be as exacting a task as
making the decisions that have been computerized.

Decisions That Can Be Modeled but Not Solved

In such cases, although we cannot find optimal solutions to the
problems modeled, we can compare solutions that are proposed by
managers or others. For example, consider the following problem
of a company that produces its product in five plants and wanted
to add a sixth plant. Each plant had a marketing region for which
it was responsible; it supplied all customers within it. Therefore,
to add a plant, the total market had to be divided into six regions
and the plant located in a region that is not otherwise served.
Once a region is specified, the optimal location of a plant within
it can be determined by available techniques. But we do not know
how to divide a large area into regions in an optimal manner.
However, by use of linear programming models we can determine
the cost of operating in any proposed regional structure. Therefore
in this case management proposed several alternative regional
structures. These were evaluated and compared by use of a model.
The results were then given to management. After studying them,
they proposed a new set of regions, and these were also compared.
The best of the proposals was then selected.

The process just described is greatly facilitated by computer-
izing the model. This accelerates the dialogue between managers
and model.

In many situations in which we can model but not solve it is possible to generate alternatives in some systematic way. For example, in the regional structuring problem we can use the following "rule" for generating alternatives: reduce the size of the region which in the last trial had the largest operating cost and enlarge the region adjacent to it that has the smallest operating cost. Such alternative-generating procedures can often be so constructed that, using information from the last trial, the next trial specified will probably (or in some cases, certainly) yield better performance than any yet obtained.

It is even possible, by use of a type of "break-even analysis," to determine when one should stop generating alternatives. For example, suppose management proposes three different regional structures of the market. After evaluation the performance measure of the best of these can be plotted as shown in Figure 5.3 over trial 1. Now suppose in trial 2 that three new proposals are similarly evaluated and the best of these is also plotted. If this process is continued, we can plot a curve through the resulting points and estimate how much improvement in performance we can expect on the next trial. When the expected improvement is no larger than the cost of making the next trial, the process should be terminated.

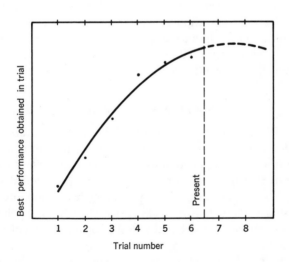

FIGURE 5.3 Break-even analysis of manager-model dialogue.

Decisions That Cannot Be Modeled

There are decisions which, because of current lack of resources or understanding, we cannot model or for which adequate models cannot be developed in time. In some of these cases the relevant manager can describe in detail how he goes about making the decision. When a manager can do so, it is possible to represent his procedure, put it on a computer, and use it in the same way as models are in the second case described above: to provide comparative evaluations. This facilitates and accelerates learning and the improvement of the model with its use. How it does so is considered in the next chapter.

There are always some decisions that cannot be modeled in any of the ways described above. These must be handled by managers as they have been in the past. Even though it is desirable to push such decisions up into one of the model-based decision-making systems, some (usually important and complex ones) will always remain at this level.

Detailed models cannot, and need not, be developed from scratch for each of the decisions that appears in the decision-flow analysis. In companies that are using the management sciences a number of these models will already be available for planners to use. For other decisions, models of which have not been developed in the company, enough work by others has been carried out and recorded in the literature to enable us to identify the relevant variables that are required in models of these decisions. This is all that is needed to take the next step.

INFORMATIONAL REQUIREMENTS

The variables that appear in a model of a decision are relevant to the decision, if the model is correct. Hence models enable us to identify the information required to make a decision. Their use assures us that no more information will be provided than is required. The importance of not providing irrelevant information to decision makers will be made apparent in the next chapter in which we consider in detail the design of management-information systems.

The design of a system to provide managers with the information that is required to do their jobs is an integral part of organizational design. It is particularly closely related to the design of systems for controlling the decisions that they have made, whether or not they have been made in the context of planning. That is, information is required not only in order to become aware of the need to make a decision and to make it but also in order to evaluate the decision once it has been made and implemented. This enables a manager to determine whether a previously made decision should be modified or corrective action should be taken.

JOBS AND DECISIONS

Once the information that is, or is believed to be, required by each decision necessary for running the firm has been specified, it is possible to group decisions in such a way as to minimize the total amount of information needed by those who have to make them; that is, decisions with identical or similar informational requirements should be put together into bundles that constitute jobs.

In some cases decisions will require more information than any one person can expect to have. In these cases the decision should be placed in the hands of a group. If this is done, it is necessary to specify how decisions are to be made by the group. Even in small groups there are many ways in which decisions can be made. A procedure for making group decisions can be completely specified by indicating whose individual approval (or disapproval) is necessary and/or sufficient for approval (or disapproval) of a decision. For example, if there are three decision makers (A, B, and C), and all their approvals are necessary for approval of a decision, then approval can only be obtained by unanimity; disapproval by any one is sufficient for disapproval by the group. Suppose A's approval is sufficient but not necessary, and the same is true for B and C. Then approval by any one is tantamount to collective approval. If any two approvals are necessary and sufficient for group approval, there is majority rule; and so on.

Making a decision is only one aspect of what might be called a decision cycle. Such a cycle has the four steps shown in Figure 5.4: *decision making, implementation, evaluation,* and *recommendation.* It does little good if, once a decision has been made, no one has responsibility for implementing it; and if implemented, it is

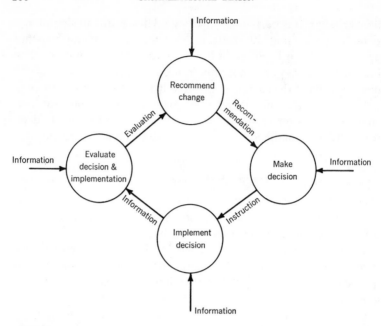

FIGURE 5.4 The decision cycle.

not evaluated; and so on. Therefore in specifying who is to make a decision it is also necessary to specify who is to perform each of the other three functions. It is clear that whoever has responsibility for implementing a decision should be responsible to those who have authority to make the decisions. Although the decision makers may want to have their decisions evaluated by someone responsible to them, higher level managers may want the evaluations submitted directly to them.

An individual manager not only makes decisions but must implement decisions made by others. He must also evaluate the decisions made by others and is responsible for making recommendations relevant to still others. Therefore, when these four phases of each decision cycle are specified, the familiar lines of authority and responsibility will emerge. Hence the organization chart is the end product, not the starting point, of organizational planning.

Additional social-psychological factors that should be taken into account in designing any job, managerial or otherwise, are discussed by F. E. Emery (1967, p. 125ff).

MEASURES AND MOTIVATION

The objectives and goals set for a manager will have little effect on his performance unless the measure of performance that is applied to him reflects these objectives and goals. Managers will try to maximize the performance measures with which their advancement and rewards are associated. If these measures are not set appropriately, they can do more to hurt overall performance of the organization than almost any other kind of error.

Consider the following caricature of an actual case, one that highlights the relevance of performance measures. It involves a department store that carries on two essential functions, buying and selling. These are handled by the purchasing and merchandising departments, respectively. The purchasing department controls the quantity of each item purchased but little else because competitive conditions largely control selection of brands. It usually buys in quantities that yield maximum quantity discounts, and hence it has little control over purchase price. This department was given the objective of minimizing the average value of inventory while meeting expected demand.

The merchandising department's main controllable variable was selling price. This price, of course, affected the amount sold. The department's objective was to maximize gross sales. The manager of this department was assisted by a statistical staff that recorded previous prices and amounts sold. From this data it put together a price-demand curve for each class of products. The staff provided estimates of the average demand supplemented by an optimistic and a pessimistic forecast (see Figure 5.5).

In planning ahead the merchandising manager had to select a price at which he would sell a product. Call this P_1. He then notified the purchasing manager of the quantity he wanted to have available. He used the price-demand curve to determine this amount. Naturally, he made an optimistic forecast (Q_1) since he did not want to risk running short. Running short would hurt his performance, but overstocking would not affect it. The purchasing manager, who had previously worked in the merchandising de-

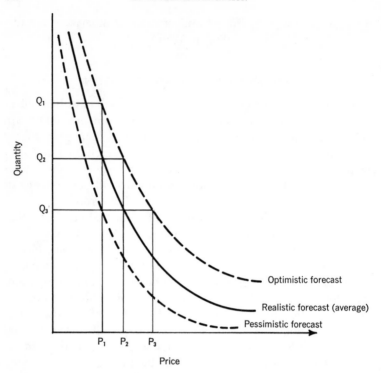

FIGURE 5.5   Price-demand curve.

partment, also had access to the price-demand curves. Knowing
the merchandising manager's practice, he read over from the
quantity Q_1 and down to the *average* demand curve. His measure
of performance required that he stock no more than the quantity
Q_2. He would so inform the merchandising manager, who would
promptly adjust his price so as to maximize gross sales, given that
only Q_2 would be available; that is, he would reset the price at P_2.
The purchasing manager would get the word and adjust his order
quantity to Q_3. As can easily be seen, if this process were to continue nothing would be bought and nothing would be sold.

   Such a state was not reached in this case because the executives
intervened and prohibited communication between the two managers. This hardly repaired a faulty set of measures of performance. A slight modification in these measures could change the

entire picture. It would involve making the purchasing department partly responsible for lost sales and the merchandising department partly responsible for excessive inventories.

Consider another case that is more typical in some respects. The company involved spent more on research and development than did all of its competitors combined, but it did not have the largest share of the relevant market. Nevertheless it was the most profitable company in its field and had enjoyed the most rapid growth of any company in its industry for several years. Its pattern of operation was as follows. Its new products were usually significantly better than what they replaced. Since the company did not have great skills in manufacturing, its production costs were relatively high. But its products were usually so superior that it could price them high enough to provide a handsome profit. These new products, however, immediately became a target for competitors who would go to work trying to find their way around the relevant patents. In time they would succeed and come up with an approximately equivalent product at a lower cost. The company involved, however, would not try to compete with lower prices; it did not have to. By that time it would either have significantly improved the product or have a new one to replace it. Thus the company's success rested almost entirely on its research and development effort.

One consequence of this pattern of growth was that the company frequently started new departments for new products and closed out old ones. This resulted in considerable movement of managerial personnel. It reached a point at which middle managers stayed in one position for less than a year on the average. The company made such shifts of managers attractive to them by salary and status rewards. But the rapid moves created a problem. Since each department was evaluated on an annual profit-and-loss basis, managers often had to be evaluated for moves without having put in a full year in their posts. To overcome this problem the company went to a quarterly evaluation of managers and their units.

Company growth began to slow up perceptibly. The reason was that managers were no longer motivated to adopt new or improved products because the time to take them from research and development and put them on the market was likely to extend beyond their tenure in their current jobs. Therefore all they would get from such adoptions were increased costs. They began to find all sorts of reasons for not taking on redesigned or new products and to concentrate on reducing manufacturing costs where they did not have great skill.

When analysis revealed the facts just described, the measures of performance were changed to include expected gains from products under development or being prepared for market. As a result the previous rate of growth was once again realized.

Theory and Measures of Performance

Deficient measures of performance must either be corrected or overcome. The theory that makes it possible to do so in an optimal way has only recently been developed. Although it is quite complex mathematically, the underlying logic is simple.

Recall that in very general terms every organization's objective is to maximize the difference between its gains and its losses. The gains and losses of an organization depend on two kinds of thing: first, those of its decisions that affect the aspects of the system under its control; second, what happens to certain uncontrolled but relevant variables. Consequently, if we can express an organization's gains and losses as a function of these variables—and this is precisely what operations research has developed some capability of doing—we can express an organization's overall objective in mathematical form. The difficulty is to find those values of the controlled variables that, under certain conditions specified by the values of the uncontrolled variables, maximize the gains minus the losses.

If this total organizational problem could be solved "all at once," a division of labor and hence organization of the effort to solve it might not be necessary because centralized control of all relevant variables would be possible in principle. In practice, however, there may be good reasons for not centralizing in this way. First, despite modern communication systems, data transmission and analysis take time and money. The assembly of all relevant information at one central point may mean that it arrives too late to be of use. Second, we cannot yet reproduce the qualitative "feel" for a problem that a good manager brings to bear on it. No one person can have this "feel" for every espect of a business; hence we may have to permit individuals and departments to become specialized. Finally every manager who uses a computer to assist him in his decision making should understand how the computations are made. He neither needs nor should desire to understand the mathematical analysis, but he should insist on much more than a statement of results: an understanding of the logic of their derivation. A manager can have this kind of understanding only in the areas of his own experience, and, because his experience is limited, he is much more likely to accept a model of the firm that is broken into parts; in other words, one that is *decomposed.*

The task of obtaining an optimal design of an organization's structure is equivalent to breaking the model of the firm into parts, each with its own measure of performance; thus, if each part is optimized exactly or approximately, the firm's optimal performance is obtained exactly or approximately. The theory of organizational structure has developed the ability to obtain optimal decompositions—that is, best structural designs—but only for fairly simple organizations as yet.

It should be noted that use of the mathematical theory of organizational structure to decompose an overall-performance measure into unit-performance measures defines a unit by a set of variables to be controlled by that unit. Hence it does not first form organizational units and then determine what measures of performance should be applied to them; it does both simultaneously. It is much more difficult, and presently impossible in most cases, to start with existing units and find out what measures of performance should be applied to them.

In addition, it will be recalled that we already suggested grouping under one manager a set of decisions that minimize his informational requirements. This is equivalent to minimizing the number of uncontrolled variables that he must take into account. It also results in considerably reduced complexity of the model which simultaneously represents all the complex decisions that he must make.

Alternatives to Restructuring

Even if we could use theory to obtain optimal reorganizations of a firm, it might not be feasible to restructure the firm if this required considerable reshuffling of responsibilities or if the groupings of tasks did not correspond to traditional groupings (e.g., if control of some purchasing and research-and-development decision variables were put together). Consequently some alternative to restructuring an organization is required to solve many, if not most, structural problems. Two such approaches have been developed, each of which works without changing the existing structure of an organization.

One approach involves the executive's ability to direct each manager to use specified values of at least some of the relevant variables not under his control. It attempts to find those values which, if used by each unit in an imperfectly structured organization in solving its problems, will yield solutions that can be assembled into at least a good approximation of the solution of the overall organizational problem. For example, to return to the department-store situation, what selling price should the executive tell the purchasing department to assume and what quantity of goods should the merchandising department be told to assume will be available? Again, the ability to answer such questions is increasing as the mathematical theory of organization develops.

The concept of "shadow prices," which is becoming familiar to many managers, emerged from the use of such an approach to organizational problems. Shadow prices are prices that an organizational unit is instructed to assume for goods or services received from another unit of the same organization. These prices may differ considerably from "true" prices, but they tend to produce unit decisions that are better from an organizational point of view than would otherwise have been made.

A third approach involves the executive's ability to set limits on the values of variables within each unit's control. It attempts to find those limits which, if used by each unit in solving its problems, will yield solutions which again can be assembled into a good approximation to the solution of the overall organizational problem. Returning to the department store, for example, what upper and lower limits should be set on the quantity stocked by the purchasing department and on the selling price set by the merchandising department? Here too ability to answer such questions is developing.

Conflict between departments is a higher level (e.g., divisional or corporate) problem, not a departmental problem, although it is usually treated departmentally. When treated as a higher level problem not only can better solutions to interdepartmental conflict be found but wear and tear on departmental managers can be significantly reduced. Consider the following case.

A decentralized manufacturing company has two divisions one of which makes a certain product that it sells to a particular market. The other division, which does not make the product, nevertheless sells it to a different market. Naturally, the corporation wanted the second division to buy the product from the first division. But the second division could often buy the product for less from competitors, and the first division could often sell all it could make at a price the second division was not willing to pay. Since both divisions were instructed to maintain a specified return on their investment and to realize a certain growth rate, if either were to give in to the other, its performance would suffer. This is fairly typical of many interdivisional pricing problems. Such problems arise out of the imposition of conflicting demands by the corporation on its divisions.

A solution was found by developing the following procedure. The corporate operations-research group was given the task of determining the lowest average price (L) at which the first division could sell the product it made and still not endanger its measure of performance. Similarly, the group determined the highest average price (H) that the second division could pay for the product and not endanger its performance. Then the following rules were applied:

1. If the second division could not buy the product from another source for less than the first division was willing to sell it for (and this could not exceed L), the second division would have to buy the product from the first.

2. If the second division could buy the product from another source for less than L, then one of two rules was applied.

2.1. If L was higher than H, and a responsible corporate executive wanted the second division to buy the product from the first division, he would have to pay the second division the difference between H and L. Thus the first division did not have to sell for less than L, and the second did not have to buy it for more than H. The corporate executive had to decide whether it was worth what he had to pay $(L - H)$ to have the sale made internally.

2.2. If L was lower than or equal to H, the second division had to buy the product from the first. If H was greater than L, then the responsible corporate executive bought the product from the first division for L and sold it to the second for H, and "kept" the difference $(H - L)$.

This procedure removed conflict between the divisions. They could cooperate fully. The decision about the relative value of interdivisional sales was where it belonged, at the corporate level. It was the corporation that now had to live with the conflict it had imposed on the divisions. It is not surprising that the corporate executive responsible for these transactions initiated a study to determine what was the value of interdivisional sales to the corporation.

The principle employed in this solution can be applied broadly to a wide variety of conflicts between organizational components.

Motivating Personnel

The presence of the right measure of performance does not assure that a manager will try as hard or do as well as he can. A motivational problem may exist. Study of motivation and performance levels of managerial and other personnel have been extensive during the last few decades (e.g., see Myers, 1964 and 1966, Cummings and Scott, 1969, and F. E. Emery, 1967). It would be inappropriate to review this large effort here. There are, however, a few observations that might fruitfully be made.

Recall the incentive scheme for salesmen that was discussed in Chapter 1. It had reduced the sale of unprofitable items and had increased the sale of profitable ones. Both the company and the salesmen benefited.

In planning, all existing incentives (even those that are implicit) should be identified and evaluated to make sure they induce behavior that is consistent with corporate objectives and goals.

We tend automatically to think of money as the only effective type of incentive, although on reflection we are aware of many other things that people want. One of the more important of these is *time*. For example, there was a study a number of years ago of a large number of female inspectors on a production line. They had failed to respond to financial incentives. A young psychologist found that most of these women were married and were working to supplement their husband's income. They had a clear idea as to how much additional family income they wanted, and more than this amount had little additional value to them. But the psychologist also found that most of them had children attending school and that the aspect of their work that most bothered them was their inability to be at home when their children returned from school. This led to the design of a time-based incentive scheme, one in which a "fair day's work" was specified. The women could leave whenever they had completed this amount of work. Productivity is reported to have more than doubled as a result of the adoption of this scheme.

Use of incentives that are rewards associated with attainment measured along relevant scales must not only be associated with the right measures but must involve the right kind of rewards. In the design of these systems psychologists and social psychologists have a major role to play.

Finally it should be noted that incentives can be used to effect the behavior of even some who are not part of the organization, but whose behavior affects its performance. It is quite common, for example, to offer incentives to suppliers for prompt delivery, or to contractors for completion of buildings on time, or to customers for large-quantity purchases. But even here there are opportunities for more creative and effective designs of incentive systems. For example, in a contract arranged with one builder his calculated profit was paid to him before work began. The client then kept all financial accounts of construction with the agreement that the client and contractor would share equally every dollar less than the estimated cost for which the building was built. Dollars over the estimated cost would yield no profit to the contractor. The client saved a significant portion of the estimated cost, and the contractor realized an equal amount in additional profit.

Recall the case discussed in Chapter 3 in which a price discount was offered by a manufacturer for advance notice of purchases from local company-operated warehouses. This offer resulted in many customers providing such notice, thereby making it possible to reduce warehouse inventories significantly.

Pricing is an incentive to customers and clearly can affect their buying behavior. What is not always so clear is what aspect of that behavior the supplier wants to control and how to do so. Research can sometimes provide the answers. In several cases it has been found that price promotions do not increase either the amount of product consumed or brand share, only the timing of purchases. In some instances this produced an artificial cycling of demand on productive facilities. This same effect on buying can be used to advantage in smoothing seasonal demand for a product.

SUMMARY

Organizational planning should be directed toward identifying the tasks required to accomplish organizational objectives, grouping them into jobs, and assigning them to individuals and groups. Responsible personnel should be provided with relevant information, appropriate measures of performance, and motivation to act in the organization's interests. A five-phase procedure can be used to accomplish these objectives.

1. *Decision-flow analysis.* This identifies each type of decision and action that is required to run an organization. It is best accomplished by preparing a flow diagram of decisions and actions that shows their precedence relations.

2. *Model construction.* Here decision models that are either available in the firm or are developed in the planning process or are available in the literature, can be used to establish decision-making procedures. If the models can be solved, the decisions can be automated or turned over to a staff; if not, a manager-model dialogue can be used to compare alternatives and hence search for one that is acceptable. Where such "objective" models are not available, the "subjective" models used by a manager can sometimes be made explicit and be used in either of the two ways mentioned. If this cannot be done, managerial judgment must be used.

3. *Informational requirements.* The uncontrolled variables in decision models specify what information is required for the decisions modeled. Where models are not available, judgment of what information is relevant must be used. Provision for informal voice communication should also be made.

4. *Decisions and jobs.* Decisions should be grouped into jobs that minimize informational requirements. Each decision should be

assigned to an individual or group; if a group, the decision-making procedure should be specified. In addition, responsibility for implementation, evaluation, and recommendation for change of each decision should be assigned.

5. *Measures and motivation.* Measures of performance should be developed for each decision maker or group that are compatible with overall organizational objectives, and hence do not produce conflict between decision makers or organizational units. Where this cannot be done, fictitious values of variables controlled by others can sometimes be specified for use with imperfect measures of performance, values that when so used yield results approximating optimal behavior from an overall organizational point of view. Alternatively it may be possible to specify ranges of values within which controlled variables can be restricted to obtain similar results. Existing incentives should be evaluated for consistency with overall objectives, and new ones should be developed where possible to encourage behavior that is efficient for these objectives.

Even an effective organization with good planning must be prepared (a) to find deficiencies in its planning and (b) to deal with the unexpected. Therefore the organization should have built into it procedures for comparing what does happen with what was expected and for taking necessary corrective action when these diverge. Such procedures are part of *control* systems, the subject of the next chapter.

Chapter 6

CONTROL

INTRODUCTION

To plan is to make decisions. Control is the evaluation of decisions, including decisions to do nothing, once they have been implemented. The process of control involves four steps:

1. Predicting the outcomes of decisions in the form of performance measures.
2. Collecting information on actual performance.
3. Comparing actual with predicted performance.
4. When a decision is shown to have been deficient, correcting the procedure that produced it and correcting its consequences where possible.

All decisions, whether made in planning or normal operations, should be subjected to control. A single control system can be applied to all decisions, whatever their origin. Therefore when planners provide a system for controlling their plan they also do so for normal operating decisions.

It should be apparent that control, decision, and management-information systems are strongly interrelated and are merely subsystems of what might be called the *management system.* These three subsystems should not be considered, let alone designed, separately. Nevertheless they frequently are. When they are treated separately, the difficulty of coordinating them is almost insurmountable; furthermore, and this is more important perhaps, the quality of the system suffers significantly.

Of the three, the design of a management-information system (MIS) is most likely to be undertaken independently of the design of the other two subsystems. Therefore let us consider such systems first; then we shall combine them with decision systems (as discussed in Chapter 5) and control systems, whose four aspects are identified above.

MANAGEMENT-INFORMATION SYSTEMS

The growing preoccupation of managers and management scientists with management-information systems is apparent. In fact some see such systems as a panacea for every type of organizational problem. Enthusiasm for such systems is understandable: it involves managers and system designers in a romantic relationship with the most glamorous instrument of our time, the electronic computer, without threatening the manager's job. Such enthusiasm is understandable, but nevertheless some of the excesses to which it has led are not.

Contrary to the impression produced by the growing literature, relatively few computerized management-information systems are actually in operation. Of those that are, many have not matched expectations, and some have been outright failures. These near and far misses could have been avoided if certain false (and usually implicit) assumptions underlying the design of many such systems had been avoided.

There seem to be five common and erroneous assumptions underlying the design of most management-information systems. Each of these is considered below.

Managers Critically Need More Relevant Information

Most management-information systems are designed on the assumption that a critical deficiency (if not the most critical) under which managers operate is the *lack of relevant information*. I do not deny that most managers lack a good deal of information that they should have, but I do deny that this is the most important informational deficiency from which they suffer. It seems to me that they suffer much more from an *overabundance of irrelevant information*.

This is not a play on words. The consequences of changing the emphasis of management-information systems from supplying relevant information to eliminating irrelevant information is considerable. If one is preoccupied with supplying relevant information, attention is almost exclusively given to the generation, storage, retrieval, and processing of data; hence emphasis is placed on constructing data banks, coding, indexing, filing, retrieval, and so on. The ideal that has emerged from this orientation is that of an infinite pool of data into which a manager could dip and pull out any information he wants. The fact is that it is more likely to be a pool in which he drowns.

If, on the other hand, one sees the manager's information problem primarily, but not exclusively, as one that arises out of an overabundance of irrelevant information, then the two most important functions of an information system become *filtration* (or evaluation) and *condensation* of information. The literature on management-information systems seldom refers to these functions, let alone considers how to carry them out.

Most managers receive much more data (if not information) than they can possibly absorb even if they spend all of their time trying to do so. Hence they already suffer from an information overload. They must spend a great deal of time separating the relevant from the irrelevant and searching for the kernels of the relevant documents. For example, I receive an average of 43 hours of unsolicited reading material per week. The solicited material is usually half again this amount.

I have seen a daily stock-status report of approximately six hundred pages of computer printout that is circulated daily across managers' desks. I have also seen requests for major capital expenditures that come in book size, several of which are distributed to managers each week. It is not uncommon for many managers to receive an average of one journal a day or more. One could go on and on.

Unless the information overload to which managers are subjected is reduced, any additional information made available by a management-information system cannot be expected to be used effectively.

Even relevant documents are usually too long. Most documents can be considerably condensed without loss of content. My point here is best made, perhaps, by describing briefly an experiment that a few of my colleagues and I conducted on the operations-research literature a few years ago. By using a panel of well-known experts we identified four recently published articles that every member of the panel considered to be "above average" and four articles that every member considered to be "below average." The authors of the eight articles were asked to prepare "objective" examinations of 30 minutes duration plus answers. These were for graduate students who were to be assigned the articles for reading. (The authors were not informed about the experiment.) Then several experienced writers were asked to reduce each article to two-thirds and one-third its original length only by eliminating words. They also prepared a brief abstract of each article. Those who did the condensing did not see the examinations to be given to the students.

A group of graduate students who had not previously read the articles were then selected. Each one was given a random selection of four articles each of which was in one of its four versions: 100, 67, or 33 percent, or abstract. Each version of each article was read by two students. All were given the same examinations. The average scores on the examinations were then compared.

For the above average articles there was no significant difference between average test scores for the 100, 67, 33 percent versions, but there was a significant decrease in the average test scores of those who had read only the abstract. For the below average articles there was no difference in average test scores among those who had read the 100, 67, and 33 percent versions, but there was a significant *increase* in the average test scores of those who read the abstract.

The sample used was obviously too small for general conclusions, but the results strongly indicate the extent to which even good writing can be condensed without loss of information. The obvious conclusion about bad writing is that its optimal length is zero.

It seems clear, then, that *condensation as well as filtration,* performed either mechanically or by hand, *should be an essential part of a management-information system,* and that *such a system should be capable of handling the unsolicited as well as solicited information that a manager receives.*

The Manager Needs the Information That He Wants

Most designers of management-information systems "determine" what information is needed by asking managers what information they would like to have. This is based on the assumption that managers know what information they need and that they want it.

For a manager to know what information he needs he must be aware of each type of decision that he should make and he must have an adequate model of each. These conditions are seldom satisfied. Most managers have some conception of at least some of the types of decision that they must make, but their conceptions of them are likely to be deficient in a very critical way. It has long been known in science that the less we understand a phenomenon, the more variables we require to explain it. Hence the manager who does not fully understand the phenomenon that he controls plays it "safe" and wants as much information as he can get. The designer, who understands the phenomenon involved less than the manager does, tries to provide more than everything. The result is an increase in the overload of irrelevant information to which management is subjected.

For example, in a case referred to in Chapter 2, market researchers in a major oil company asked their marketing managers what variables they thought were relevant in estimating the sales volume of future service stations. Almost 70 variables were identified. The market researchers then added about half as many variables and performed a large multiple regression analysis of sales of existing stations against these variables and found about 35 to be "statistically significant." A forecasting equation was based on this analysis. Later an operations-research team constructed a model based on only one variable, perceived lost time of the customer, which predicted sales better than the 35-variable regression equation. The "significance" of 33 of the 35-variables was explained by their effect on such perception.

The moral is simple: *one cannot specify what information is needed for decision making until an explanatory model of the decision process and the system involved in it has been constructed and tested.* Information systems are subsystems of management systems. They cannot be designed adequately without taking decision making and control into account.

Give a Manager What Information He Needs and His Decision Making Will Improve

It is frequently assumed that, if a manager is provided with the information he needs, then he will have no problem in using it effectively. There is a good deal of evidence to the contrary. For

TABLE 6.1 A Production-Sequencing Problem

Product No.	Time Required on Machine	
	M_1	M_2
1	7	18
2	3	13
3	12	9
4	14	5
5	20	8
6	4	16
7	2	20
8	9	15
9	19	1
10	6	13

example, the following is about as "simple" a problem in production management as one can find. There are 10 products to be made, each requiring time on two machines, M_1 and M_2. Each product must first go to M_1 and then to M_2. The problem is to find the order in which to produce the 10 items that will require the least possible time to complete all the products. Simple enough. All the information required to solve the problem is given in Table 6.1.

Despite the fact that this problem is much less complicated than most real production-management problems, and despite the fact that all of the data required to solve it are provided, very few managers can solve it. They cannot do it by trying the alternatives because there are more than $3\frac{1}{2}$ million of them. Yet the problem can be solved in less than a minute *if one knows how*.

Take the product with the lowest time entry in the table, No. 9. Since the entry (1) appears in the right-hand column, place this product last in the sequence and cross out line 9 in the table. Take the product with the lowest remaining time entry, No. 7. Since the entry (2) appears in the left-hand column, place this product first in the sequence and cross out line 7. Take the product with the lowest remaining time entry, No. 2. Since the entry (3) appears in the left-hand column, place No. 2 second from the left (after No. 7) and cross out line 3. Continue coming in from the left for left-hand column entries and from the right for right-hand column entries until all the products have been placed in order. In case of a tie, either may be selected.

The point of this example is that, if we know how to use required information to solve a problem, we can either program it for a computer or for a person whose time is less valuable than a manager's. If we do not know how to solve the problem, there is no assurance that having the required information will help.

In most management problems there are too many possible solutions to expect judgment or intuition to select the best one, even if provided with perfect information. Furthermore, when probabilities (uncertainties) are involved in a problem, the unguided mind has difficulty in aggregating them in a valid way. There are many "simple" problems involving probabilities in which untutored intuition usually does very badly; for example, what are the correct odds that at least 2 out of 25 people selected at random will have their birthdays on the same day of the year? They are better than even.

The moral: *it is necessary to determine how well managers can use needed information.* If they cannot use it well, they should be provided either with decision rules or with feedback on their performance so that they can identify and learn from their mistakes. More on this point later.

More Communication Means Better Performance

One characteristic of most management-information systems is that they provide managers with more current information about what other managers and their units are doing. The underlying belief is that better interdepartmental communication enables managers to coordinate their decisions more effectively and, therefore, that it improves overall performance of the organization. Not only is this not necessarily so, but it seldom is so. One would hardly expect two competing companies to become more cooperative if each was provided with more and better information about the other. This analogy is not as far fetched as one might at first suppose. Departments and divisions of a corporation often compete with each other more intensely than they do with other companies. Recall the department store example used in the last chapter. Perfect communication between the purchasing and merchandising managers in that situation could result in nothing being bought and nothing being sold. Survival of the store required that communication between them be restricted.

When organizational units have inappropriate measures of performance that put them into conflict with each other, as is more often the case than not, communication between them may hurt overall performance, not help it. *Organizational structure and performance measures should be put right before opening the flood gates and permitting free flow of information between parts of the organization.*

A Manager Does Not Have to Know How an Information System Works, Only How to Use It

Most designers of management-information systems seek to make their systems innocuous and unobstructive to managers, to avoid frightening them. The designers try to provide managers with very easy access to the system and to assure them that they need know nothing more about it. The designers usually succeed in keeping managers from knowing any more about it. This leaves managers unable to evaluate the system as a whole. It often makes them afraid even to try to do so less they display their ignorance publicly. In failing to evaluate their management-information systems, managers delegate much of their control of the organization to the system's designers, who may have many virtues, but managerial competence is seldom among them.

Recall the case of the computerized production-control system that was discussed in the last chapter. That system cost the involved company about $150,000 per month more than the hand-operated system it had replaced, exclusive of the cost of the computer. Management had been unable to find this out because it did not understand the system well enough to ask relevant questions of it. The relevant questions were obvious and simple.

The moral: *no management-information system should ever be installed unless the managers it serves understand how it operates well-enough to evaluate its performance.* Managers must control the computer, not be controlled by it.

AN INTEGRATED MANAGEMENT SYSTEM

Avoidance of the five deficiencies we have just considered requires (*a*) designing an information system as a subsystem, as an

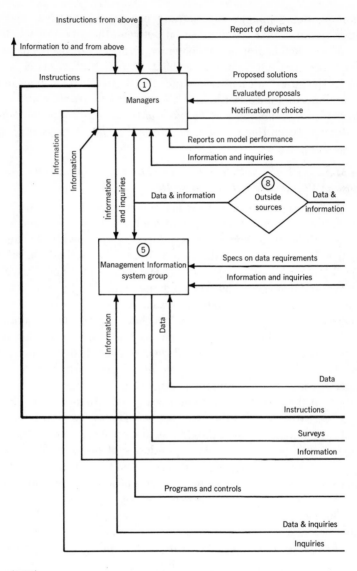

Legend
 A computerizable activity

FIGURE 6.1 An adaptive management system.

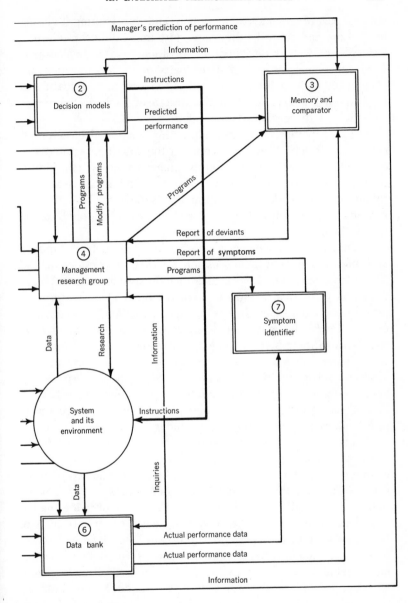

FIGURE 6.1.

integral part of a management system, and thus relating it closely to decision and control subsystems; (*b*) imbedding the information system in a redesigned organization, one in which performance objectives and goals of parts of the organization are compatible with each other and overall objectives and goals; and (*c*) involving management in the design of each of these subsystems and the organization itself.

Up to this point we have considered information, decisions, and control separately. Now let us consider them in an integrated system, one that constitutes an adaptive management system. Figure 6.1 is a schematic diagram of such a system. In the discussion that follows we will work our way around this diagram. The numbers heading the paragraphs below refer to the corresponding boxes in the diagram.

1. In this system *managers* receive instructions from "above" and information from numerous sources that we consider below. The instructions that they receive include specification of objectives and goals that are to be pursued, and related measures of performance. With these inputs management either (*a*) makes decisions directly, when no models are available, and then issues instructions to the system managed, where they are implemented; or (*b*) enters into a dialogue with the appropriate decision models. These models may either be in a computer or they may be hand-operated by a management-research group. We have already considered the nature of such a dialogue. It consists of managers proposing alternative solutions of a problem to a model. The model performs a comparative evaluation of these proposals and feeds the results back to the managers who may either select one or continue the dialogue until either satisfaction is reached or time runs out. Eventually managers make a decision, issue instructions to the system, and "notify" the model of the choice once it is made.

2. The *decision models* involved in such a system are of two types: those from which best solutions can be derived and those that can be used only to compare alternatives. In the first case the model generates a solution to the problem by itself, using information supplied to it by the information system and it issues instructions derived from the solution directly to the system. It also predicts the performance to be expected and "sends" this to the memory.

When a manager makes a choice based on a dialogue with the model, he so notifies the model, which then predicts the outcome in performance-measurement terms and sends this prediction to the memory. When managers make a decision without the use of a model, *they* predict the outcome and send this to the memory. The memory should receive a prediction of performance for every decision that is made regardless of how it is made.

3. The *memory* (which may or may not be computerized) retains the predictions of performance until it receives information on actual performance from the data bank. It then *compares* actual and predicted performance and where these are found to diverge significantly it reports this as a *deviant*. A report of deviants is sent to managers for those decisions that they have made without the use of models, and a similar report is sent to the management-research group for decisions that were made by using models.

4. The *management research group* consists of management scientists who have the responsibility for developing decision models, for programming their use, and for designing and programming the memory and comparator. This group attempts to find the causes of deviations of predicted from actual performance when models have been involved. Since deviations can be caused either by faulty information or by faulty models, this group must find which is the cause and correct it. If this group fails to find an explanation for a deviation it withdraws the relevant model from use until it or the informational input is repaired, and so notifies management. In these cases managers then resume decision making until the relevant models are once again usable. In some cases managers can provide the management-research group with an explanation of the deviation.

Note that the decision and control loop just described is *adaptive;* it learns from its own mistakes and is self-correcting.

The management-research group also has responsibility for setting up a symptom identifier, which we discuss below.

In analyzing management decisions and developing models for them the management-research group determines what information is required for decision making and so notifies the management-information-system group.

5. The *management-information-system group* has responsibility for designing and operating the management-information sys-

tem. It receives information from all parts of the system, solicited and unsolicited, including information originally received by other parts of the system, solicited or not. The management-information system group processes such information (including filtration and condensation), and provides output where it is needed. The system that this group operates includes a data bank.

6. The *data bank* is either a computerized or hand-operated system that collects, processes, stores, retrieves, and disseminates information on a regular basis or on special request (inquiry) from any part of the system.

Note that managers, management researchers, and information system specialists all can obtain information directly from the data bank and the system being managed. They also receive information from *outside sources* (8).

7. Up to this point we have only considered how problems that have been identified are solved, but not how problems are identified. A complete decision cycle consists of three stages:

a. Identification of symptoms.

b. Diagnosis.

c. Prescription.

Prescription, of course, is decision making—the transformation of information into instruction—which we have considered in detail. Diagnosis is what is involved in developing explanatory decision models. This is a principal activity of the management-research group. But symptom and problem identification have not yet been discussed.

A symptom is a deviation of a system's behavior from what is considered to be "normal." For example, a fever is an abnormally high temperature. Blood pressure may be above or below the normal range. Similarly, when inventories become larger than normal, it is a sign of something wrong. Costs lower than usual are also symptoms, but not necessarily of something wrong. However, they do indicate a change in the system that requires attention.

A complete technology is available for defining "normality" of a system's behavior and for detecting deviations from it. The technology is that of *statistical quality control*. It is normally applied to performance characteristics of production subsystems, but it need not be so restricted. By statistical analysis of past performance of a system it is possible to define a range of "normal" behavior. Behavior outside this range is very unlikely to occur unless the system has changed in some fundamental way. Hence such behavior is taken as a symptom of something wrong. The probability that something is wrong when a symptom occurs can be set at any level that is desired.

By applying statistical techniques to a wide variety of performance measures of a system we can detect when something has probably gone wrong, and direct diagnostic attention to it. Once the symptom-identification procedure has been developed (e.g., one that uses a statistical control chart), its use can be computerized. On receipt of information about actual performance from the data bank the computer can carry out the necessary analyses and report any deviation from normal behavior.

Symptoms are obtained not only by comparing current behavior of the system with its past behavior but also by comparing its current behavior with that of similar systems; for example, with that of competitors. A company that is not growing as fast as are most of its competitors has something wrong with it. Such comparisons can also be programmed for the computer.

It is possible to go even further in symptom identification by dealing with *presymptoms*. A presymptom is a predictor of a future symptom. For example, when a person says that he feels as though he were going to be ill, he has observed a presymptom. These are not mysterious premonitions but explainable phenomena. Normal behavior is not fixed but fluctuates within a range, a range that defines it. These fluctuations are usually random in character. It is a presymptom for normal behavior to become nonrandom. For example, we may observe a series of cost figures (obtained over consecutive weeks), all of which are within the range of normality but each of which is above average, or they may show a trend within that range. In these cases nonrandom behavior has been observed, behavior that indicates a possible change in the system or its environment. Such a change should receive attention.

Tests for nonrandomness are well developed and can be conducted by a computer.

Consider the case of a company whose raw material is bought on the commodity exchange and hence is subject to daily price fluctuations. The company was naturally interested in determining when these prices had gone out of control in either direction.

Analysis of past data on prices of the commodity indicated that in most periods preceding a deviation of price from normal, non-random price fluctuations had occurred. Using this information it was possible to predict when prices would go out of control and in which direction, seven weeks earlier than had previously been possible. This enabled the company to adjust its buying of the commodity.

Note that such symptom- and presymptom-identification systems as have been described can be programmed to report only unusual behavior; that is, to provide only "exception reports." Hence irrelevant information can be kept to a minimum.

The management system I have described applies to any level of management. The linkage between levels is apparent. Each level receives instructions from above and supplies those above with information. Lower levels of management are included in the system controlled at each level. Even top management may receive instructions from external sources, the stockholders or the government. Hence a total corporate design may consist of a hierarchy of interlocking management systems of the type described. (A generalized form of such a hierarchy is discussed by Beer, 1968.)

SUMMARY

Control is the evaluation of decisions after they have been implemented. It involves predicting the outcome of a decision, comparing it with the actual outcome, and taking corrective action where the match is poor. Control systems should be attached to every decision-making system. But each decision-making system requires an information system to provide the necessary inputs. These three systems—decision, control, and information—combine to make a management system.

In designing a management-information system there are five assumptions (one or more of which are often made implicitly) that should be avoided unless they are critically examined and found valid. These are the following:

1. Managers critically need more relevant information. (They usually have a greater need for a reduction of irrelevant information.)

2. Managers need the information that they want. (This is true only if they have good models of their decisions. If they do, they need not make the decisions at all. Others or computers can do so.)

3. If a manager is given the information he needs, his decision making will improve. (This is true in general only for very simple decisions, but not for the more numerous complex ones.)

4. More communication among managers leads to better performance. (This is true only in organizations whose unit objectives are nonconflicting and compatible with those of the organization as a whole.)

5. A manager does not have to know how his information system works, only how to use it. (If he does not, he will be controlled by it—not in control of it.)

Avoidance of these five assumptions requires imbedding an information system in a management system, in whose design management is involved, and taking steps to ensure the compatibility of unit objectives with those of the organization as a whole. A management system should involve managers, management scientists, and information-system specialists in close and continuous collaboration, all exploiting the potentialities of computers where possible. Such a system should be capable of identifying problems when they arise as well as solving already recognized ones, and of learning from its own mistakes.

We turn now to a brief and final discussion of some organizational aspects of the planning process itself.

Chapter 7

ORGANIZING THE PLANNING EFFORT

INTRODUCTION

The conception of corporate planning that has been developed in this book clearly involves managers, management scientists, and information-system specialists in a continuing collaborative effort. The success of the effort depends more on the relationship between them than on anything else.

It will be recalled that in adaptive planning the process of planning is considered to be more important than its product. Management has more to gain by participating in this process than in consuming a plan that has been produced by others. Therefore involvement of managers in the planning process is essential for effective planning.

In this concluding chapter we first examine several important implications of this concept of planning. We do so by considering three questions:

1. Where should planning be located in the organizational structure?

2. How much time should managers spend in planning?

3. How should managers not involved in planning, and others significantly affected by plans, be kept informed of progress in planning?

The second problem considered in this chapter is primarily relevant to large organizations, particularly those involved in diverse activities at many different locations. Comprehensive planning in such organizations requires coordination of planning in many locations at different levels. How can such coordination best be obtained?

Finally we consider the characteristics one would like to have in a planning group collectively and in its members individually.

MANAGEMENT INVOLVEMENT IN PLANNING

Most managers do some planning but usually on their own and not in a systematic or comprehensive way. In order to plan systematically and comprehensively the planning process must itself be organized and efficiently managed and carried out. It has seemed natural, therefore, to many executives who recognize the need for an organized planning effort to create corporate and/or divisional, or departmental planning units.

If a unit of this type is given complete responsibility for preparing a plan and for submitting it for approval by managers, then in most cases planning has been given the kiss of death. The probability of success of a planning effort decreases as the organizational autonomy of the planning activity increases. Such autonomy ensures the noninvolvement of line managers and often of executives as well. Personnel who are considered to be unsuited for more "productive" activity are usually assigned to such units. They often become isolation chambers for researchers as well as for ex-managers and staff personnel, within which they can be assured of no or little relevant contact with the reality being planned for. Such units often have a role like that of witch doctors in primitive tribes; they officiate over rituals that have little effect on people once the ritual has been completed, and no effect on the objective situation.

These comments are not meant to imply that there should not be a planning staff, only that it should not have the sole responsibility for planning. It should have responsibility for participating in and supporting the planning activities of managers. On the other hand, these comments do imply that a planning activity should not be launched by creating a formal planning function and turning the job over to it.

In my opinion the General Electric Company's use of planning task forces is about as successful a way of *launching* a planning effort as I have seen or been involved in. (In general this company has not been as successful in keeping the efforts, once launched, afloat.) I have participated in two such efforts. The first was in the Lamp Division in 1953–1954, an activity to which I have already referred. This task force was chaired by a member of the administrative staff of the vice president and general manager of the division. It is not a mere coincidence that the task force's chairman was Fred J. Borch, now chairman and chief executive officer of the company. The other members were the home office manager in charge of sales districts, the home office manager in charge of lamp assembly, the home office manager of the division's distribution network, the manager of the division's chemical plant, the manager of one of its glass plants, the manager of its manufacturing development program, the chief patent counsel, and the head of the division's auditing staff. This group of managers was supplemented by three professional operations-research workers.

The chairman and the auditor, together with the technical staff, began to work full time on the problem. They met with the other members of the task force on a two-day-per-week schedule. This soon increased to three days per week and in the final stages of the project (which lasted about 15 months) to eight days per week.

The second planning task force on which I served was in the Appliance Division in the late 1950s. This task force involved five managers and two operations researchers, but this group worked for about 18 months. This task force was chaired by one of the members of the earlier Lamp Division task force.

In both of these planning efforts large amounts of the time of the best managers in the divisions were committed to the activities.

Maintenance and control of these plans, once accepted, were turned over to management-research groups. But managers were not as involved in this process as they should have been. The need for continuous planning was not appreciated. Comprehensive and detailed planning was thought of as something that is done only on occasion.

It would have been desirable in these cases if smaller groups of managers and researchers, rotated periodically in such a way as to have an "experienced core" at all times, had been established to update and extend the plan on a continuing basis.

There is no doubt that the time spent by the managers in these efforts contributed significantly to the development of their managerial skills.

Since these task-force experiences I have been involved in a number of planning efforts, each organized differently, but all involving large commitments of management time supplemented by that of researchers. The most successful single arrangement in which I have been involved grew out of organizational changes produced by an operations-research study. In this study of a major functional activity of a corporation it was concluded that the function should be headed by two vice presidents: a senior vice president responsible for strategy and long-range planning, and a junior vice president responsible for tactics and short-range planning. A single research staff was set up to serve both. Other managers reporting to the two vice presidents were involved in both tactical and strategic planning. In this case planning was never directed toward producing a plan; planning was, and continues to be, an ongoing process. Management planning and research are completely welded together, and no effort is made to distinguish between them. This is a consequence of the conception of planning as a continuing responsibility of all managers and not as a sometime activity, usually associated with crises.

The organizational problem of planning therefore consists of finding ways to make it an integral part of management and management-research processes; not how to set up a separate planning unit. Once this has been appreciated, productive planning can be initiated.

Ideally the group responsible for planning (managers plus researchers) should report directly to the executive who has final authority over the planning process. He should serve as head of the group, even if it is necessary for him to delegate daily direction of it to another. In my opinion, the planning group, however composed, should not report to a manager who in turn reports to the responsible executive. For example, it is quite common to have a planning unit report to a financial executive who is not the ultimate decision maker on planning even though he may be a member of the management committee that accepts or rejects plans. Such a practice tends to give planning a financial bias. People from finance should be involved in corporate planning, but they should have no more control over it than has any other functional group.

PLANNING STAFF

Planning cannot and should not be done exclusively by managers; they require technical support. However, as I have indicated, I do not believe that the staff should be identified and organized into a corporate planning department. There is no profession of corporate planners. The skills required for support of effective planning must be drawn from a variety of professions such as operations research, information-system sciences, economics, statistics, behavioral sciences, and other management-related fields. Those professions used in planning are better drawn from management service groups in the organization and are better organized as a task force. This has several advantages. Such persons have no vested interest in, and hence will not be defensive of, previous planning efforts. Therefore they will usually have a fresher approach to planning than those labeled as planners. Second, they disseminate a concern with planning back in the units from which they come and hence encourage and accelerate the development in these units of efforts that support planning.

If qualified staff for planning is not available within the company, such support can be obtained from "outside" sources. Consulting firms or academic research groups can provide personnel who can work with managers in the planning process. (This is what the General Electric Company did in the two task forces described above.) But two cautions are necessary here. First, planning itself should not be contracted out. Remember that successful planning cannot be done *to* or *for* an organization; it can only be done *by* the organization itself. Second, the outside staff should be given responsibility for on-the-job training of company personnel in planning staff work. Without such trained personnel within the company, the outside experts will leave a vacuum behind them, an inability to maintain a plan and sustain the planning process.

If there is a specially designated planning department, it should, in my opinion, report to a manager in charge of what might be called "management services." Operations research, information systems, and related groups should also report to him. With this arrangement personnel can at least be circulated among the units containing relevant types of expert.

The director of management services and the senior staff personnel engaged in planning should have a deep and broad understanding of management's problems. In order to acquire such understanding they should participate in management's discussions of its problems whether or not they are working on them. They should be as integral a part of the executive function as managers are. Unless planning-staff members are taken into management's councils they cannot perceive the needs, desires, and constraints under which management operates and hence cannot be responsive to them.

In one organization with which I am familiar top management conducts regularly scheduled briefing sessions for its entire planning, research, and systems staff in order to keep them up to date and involved. This procedure works·well but should be supplementary to, not a substitute for, direct involvement of senior planning personnel in management's decision-making sessions.

INVOLVEMENT OF OTHERS IN PLANNING

The managers not directly involved in planning, and other personnel (e.g., staff) significantly affected by it should be kept informed about what is going on. They should be exposed to the philosophy, strategy, and methodology of planning, as well as to the underlying assumptions and data-collection and analytical procedures. If this is done, when results are obtanied they will not come as a surprise and hence can be implemented with less fuss than would otherwise be the case.

In planning for General Electric's Lamp Division the nature and purpose of planning were made known to key personnel. Members of the planning group met separately with most managers in the division to explain the work and to solicit suggestions. As many as possible were involved in the planning process where their particular experience and expertise were relevant. The cooperation proved to be invaluable during the planning process. Fears of a "shakeup" were allayed, and this allowed the division to continue to operate at a high level of efficiency. As a result the plan that was produced received the almost unanimous support of management and staff.

MULTILEVEL AND MULTIUNIT PLANNING

In an organization that operates at multiple levels with multiple units at the same or different levels—that is, where the pyramid is high and broad—planning usually has to be carried out simultaneously at most, if not all, levels. The need for coordination of planning at different levels is too obvious to require discussion. But what is not so obvious is that a corporate plan should not be an adjusted aggregation of plans prepared by divisions, departments, or other parts of the organization. Plans prepared by subunits for aggregation at the top tend to be propaganda for a larger share of corporate resources. To be sure, effective corporate planning requires planning in every part of the organization, but it should be coordinated methodologically and conceptually from the top.

It is not easy to obtain the required coordination of planning efforts at multiple levels and in multiple units. In my opinion such coordination can best be obtained by a system of *planning review boards*.

PLANNING REVIEW BOARDS

Consider a typical three-level multiunit planning organization such as is shown in Figure 7.1. For the moment let us concentrate on the divisional (middle) level. Planners at this level have significant inputs to make to departmental planning and require inputs from corporate planning if they are to function effectively. They also have inputs to make at the corporate level and inputs to receive from the departmental level. Planning at any intermediate

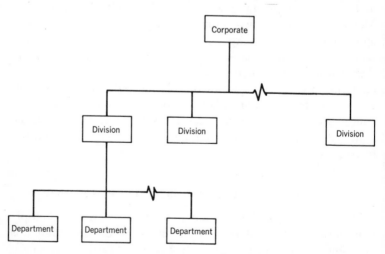

FIGURE 7.1   Three-level organization of planning units.

level requires understanding of planning both above and below it, as well as understanding of the planning of other units at the same level. The latter is necessary if plans made in different units at the same level are to be compatible.

Dissemination of the necessary information and development of the necessary understanding can be obtained by establishing planning review boards for each planning unit. These boards should establish policies that the units follow and evaluate the processes and product of these units.

Planning review boards should be composed as follows: (a) The head of each planning unit—the senior manager in the unit at that level—is a member of the board to which his planning unit reports. This board should also contain (b) the head of each planning unit under him, and (c) the senior manager at the level above him, who serves as chairman of that board.

It follows, therefore, that each intermediate-level manager is a member of boards at three levels:

1. The board to which his superior reports.
2. The board to which he reports, chaired by his superior.
3. The board of each of his "inferiors," which he chairs.

Figure 7.2 shows this structure.

One critical aspect of such an organization for planning should be noted. It can only work if the span of control of each manager is restricted to no more than about seven other managers. The reasons for this are too obvious to discuss, but it should be observed that there are many other good reasons for limiting the span of control.

At the lowest level of management the boards can consist of representative nonmanagerial personnel selected in some way appropriate to the situation. At the highest level a board of directors normally exists already. This board should also serve as a planning review board at the corporate level and when doing so should include those planning heads that report to the chief executive officer.

Activities of the Planning Review Board

In the early stages of planning this board can play an important role in identifying and defining the deficiencies in the operation

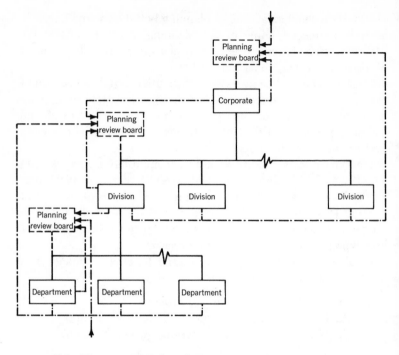

FIGURE 7.2   Planning-review-board system.

and activities of their organizaton. Managers so frequently have to "sell" their organization and hence enumerate its virtues that they seldom have the time or the inclination to identify its deficiencies and seek any underlying causes of them.

In one very successful company the chairman of the board, the president, and the executive vice president were asked to identify the deficiencies of their company in a planning review session, and took about four hours to do so. There was no complete agreement among them, but the discussion of their points of disagreement had great value for the planners present. When finished they had formulated 14 deficiencies, which they ranked in order of importance. This list has been used ever since by them in evaluating the planning process.

The planning review board should critically review every aspect of the work of the planners. Its members should press for explicit formulation of assumptions; challenge the accuracy, reliability, and meaning of data; the uses to which they are put; and also question the validity of models and the solutions derived from them. They should also try to ensure the comprehensiveness of the planning effort and see to it that account is taken of all significant interactions between parts of the plan.

The board should also play a constructive role. It should be responsible for formulating stylistic objectives and constraints and for constructing appropriate measures of performance. It should suggest alternative courses of action, programs, and policies that should be explored by planners.

When plans have been accepted, the board should oversee their implementation and continuously review their performance. Its members should suggest revisions in the content of the plan or in implementation procedures where appropriate.

Executives and managers on planning review boards are usually quite aware of deficiencies in their knowledge and understanding of aspects of the business and its environment. In such cases I have found it useful to arrange seminars and discussion sessions to which one or more inside or outside experts are invited. Topics for some recent sessions of this type include (a) the urban race problem, (b) international conflict, (c) the money market, (d) changing trends in labor-management relations, and (e) the problem of corporate size. In such sessions a problem area can be thoroughly probed by managers and experts. They often lead to specific researches in support of the planning effort.

CONCLUSION

I conclude on the same note with which I began. The value of planning to managers lies more in their participation in the process than in their consumption of its product. Such participaton stimulates the development of a deeper understanding of the business and its environment, and it forces the systematic formulation and evaluation of alternatives that would not otherwise be considered. It unleashes large amounts of creativity that is so often suppressed by routine and the need to respond to crises.

More than 2000 years ago Sun Tzu (400–320 B.C.) perceived the value of planning, and it has not changed since:

> With many calculations, one can win;
> with few one cannot. How much less chance of
> victory has one who makes none at all!
> *The Art of War, i*

APPENDIX: MODELS

An Example of Model Construction

The following is a very elementary example of model construction that is intended to give those unfamiliar with the process some feeling for it. The situation with which it deals is that of an operator of a newsstand, about as simple a business as one can imagine. To simplify it even further we deal with a small-town operator who sells only one newspaper, which has only one edition each day.

The operator buys a certain number n of newspapers from the publisher. He pays an amount a for each paper. He sells papers for an amount b that is greater then a (i.e., $b > a$). Therefore his profit per paper sold is $(b - a)$.

When he returns an unsold paper to the publisher, he receives an amount c that is less than a (i.e., $a > c$). Therefore his loss per paper returned is $(a - c)$.

Let d represent the number of papers he could sell on any day if he had an unlimited supply. Then he may sell less than d if the number he buys (n) is less than d (i.e., if $n < d$). If he buys more than d, he will sell d papers and return $(n - d)$.

The demand d varies from day to day. Let $p(d)$ represent the probability that demand will be equal to d on any one day. Then, since d cannot be less than zero nor more than infinity, the sum of $p(d)$ for values of d from zero to infinity must be equal to 1.0. Hence

$$\sum_{d=0}^{\infty} p(d) = 1.0,$$

where

$$\sum_{d=0}^{\infty} p(d)$$

is the sum of the probabilities of d over the range from zero to infinity.

The problem of the operator is to determine an amount of papers (n^*) to order each day so that his average daily profit P is maximized.

Summarizing the situation:

139

1. Measure of performance:
    $$P = \text{average daily profit}.$$
2. Controlled variable:
    $$n = \text{number of papers bought per day}.$$
3. Uncontrolled variables:
    $a =$ cost per paper brought,
    $b =$ price per paper sold,
    $c =$ salvage value per paper returned,
    $d =$ demand on a particular day,
    $p(d) =$ probability that d papers could be sold on a randomly selected day (if supply were not limiting).

Now we can construct a model to represent the situation and the decision required in it.

On days on which the number of papers purchased, n, is less than or equal to demand d — that is, $n \leqslant d$ — the operator sells n papers and this earns $n(b-a)$. The average profit over all such days is

$$\sum_{d=0}^{d=n} n(b-a)\,p(d).$$

On days on which the number of papers purchased (n) is more than demand d (i.e., $n > d$) the operator sells d papers, returns $(n-d)$, and thus takes in $d(b-a)$ as income but loses $(n-d)(a-c)$. Therefore the average profit over all such days is

$$\sum_{d=n+1}^{\infty} [d(b-a) - (n-d)(a-c)]\,p(d).$$

Therefore average daily profit is given by

$$P = \sum_{d=0}^{d=n} n(b-a)\,p(d) + \sum_{d=n+1}^{\infty} [d(b-a) - (n-d)(a-c)]p(d).$$

The only constraint is that the number of papers purchased be not less than zero; that is, n must be greater than or equal to zero: $n \geqslant 0$.

The problem can now be formulated as that of finding a value of n (n^{*}), the number of papers to be bought, which maximizes the average daily profit P, subject to the constraint that n^{*} is nonnegative. Once the numerical values of the uncontrolled variables are known, this problem can be easily solved.

Example of Use of a Model

The model described here has been used by a chemical company in its strategic planning. The mathematics involved are quite complex, but I use graphics to represent the relevant relationships between variables.

The questions to which the model was addressed were the following:

1. How much should the company spend anually on Research and Development (R&D)?
2. How should it divide this amount between expenditures on *offensive* and *defensive* research?

"Offensive research" was defined as that directed toward producing new sources of income for the company; "defensive research," as that directed toward protecting existing sources of income through product and process improvements.

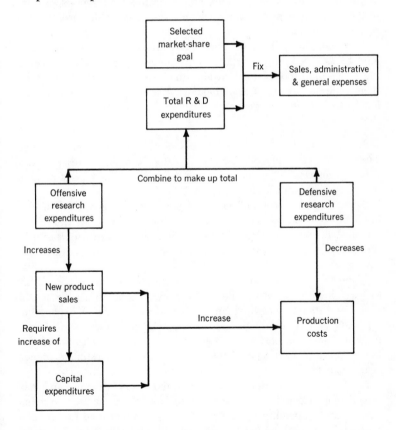

FIGURE A.1   Conceptual model of effects of expenditures on R & D.

The offensive-defensive classification of research projects suggested a conceptual model that, when modified by analysis of the system and performance records, appeared as shown in Figure A.1.

In turn this model suggested a measure of performance that, when tempered by company practices and data availability, came out as

return on gross value of plant = (sales revenue
— production costs — sales, administrative, and general expenses
— R&D cost)/gross value of plant.

By recombining the components of this measure in various ways a wide variety of performance measures could be obtained. Hence results using different measures could be compared before management selected the one that it wished to use.

The reason for grouping sales, administrative, and general expenses in the measure of performance lies in a data-availability problem that is discussed below.

The mathematical model that was extracted from the conceptual model was based on four relationships between the variables shown in the conceptual model, relationships that were first hypothesized and then confirmed by use of available data. For our purposes here it is sufficient to indicate the general nature of these relationships and how they were used.

1. An estimate of next year's sales of old products was prepared. Then a trial value of dollars to be allocated to offensive research next year was selected. This trial value was then used in the type of relationship shown graphically in Figure A.2.

Sales in any one year, of course, depend on offensive research done in a number of preceding years. A set of numerical weights were found for offensive-research expenditures in preceding years (decreasing as they went back) so as to minimize the errors of the estimates of new sales.

Using the trial value of offensive research for next year and adding the weighted cumulative offensive-research expenditures up to this year, one obtains a weighted cumulative offensive-research expenditure for next year. When this is used in the relationship shown in Figure A.2, an estimate of next year's "new" sales is obtained. This is added to the estimate of next year's "old" sales to obtain an estimate of next year's total sales.

2. A trial value of dollars to be allocated to defensive research next year is then selected and converted into a weighted cumulative defensive-research expenditure in a manner similar to that used for offensive research. The resulting figure, together with the estimate of next year's

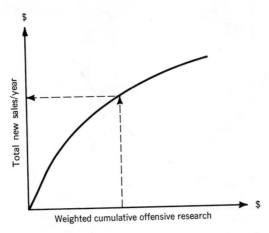

FIGURE A.2   Total "new" sales per year as a function of weighted cumulative offense research expenditures.

total sales obtained in step 1, are used in the relationship shown in Figure A.3 to obtain an estimate of next year's production costs.

3. The estimate of total sales for next year is then used to obtain an estimate of the gross value of plant required for next year with the help of the type of relationship shown in Figure A.4. Since the current value of the plant is known, it can be subtracted from the estimated

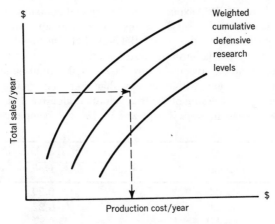

FIGURE A.3   Estimation of next year's production costs for an estimate of next year's total sales.

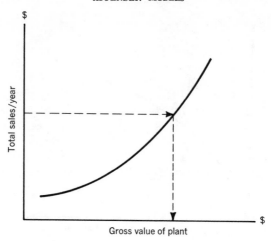

FIGURE A.4   Estimate of gross value of plant required to produce estimated total sales for next year.

gross value to obtain an estimate of the capital expenditures that are required for next year.

4. It was not possible to allocate selling costs of previous years to old and new products, nor was it possible to find a suitable relationship between R&D expenditures and selling costs. After internal sources of data were explored thoroughly without useful results, attention was turned to external sources of (industry) data. A source was found in which total annual R&D expenses and aggregated annual sales, administrative, and general (SAG) expenses were available from sixteen chemical companies for the period 1947–1957. From this data the following descriptive relationships were found:

The variances of the average ratios shown in the right-hand column were significantly less within groups than between groups. Consequently, using (a) the sum of the trial values of offensive and defensive research employed in steps 1 and 2, and (b) the company's market

Market Share (percent)	Average R & D Dollars/Year / SAG Dollars/Year
0.2–0.5	0.20
0.5–2.0	0.22
2.0–4.0	0.27
4.0+	0.36

share objective for next year, one can obtain an estimate of SAG expenses for next year.

5. Estimates of each component of the measure of performance are now available and hence it can be computed.

6. By varying (a) the trial values of offensive research expenditures for next year, (b) the trial values of defensive research expenditures for next year, and (c) the market share objective, one can obtain a set of values of the estimated return on gross plant for each. This can of course be done by a computer. From the return function that is obtained in this way the combination of the three variables manipulated that yields the greatest expected return can be selected.

REFERENCES AND BIBLIOGRAPHY

What follows is not a comprehensive bibliography on corporate planning. A good recent approximation to this can be found in Steiner (1969). The books and articles listed are either referred to in the text or are ones that have contributed to or stimulated my thinking on the subject. The notes on the entries are intended to help the reader decide where to go from here.

Ackoff, R. L., *Scientific Method: Optimizing Applied Research Decisions*, Wiley, New York, 1962.

A detailed exposition of optimizing methodology as it applies to the solution of individual problems.

————, "Towards an Idealized University" *Management Science*, **15** (1968), B121–B131.

The design of a university from which the discussion of learning cells (in Chapter 3) is taken. It covers other pedagogical techniques and other-than-pedagogical functions of a university.

————, "Beering and Branching through Corporate Planning," to appear in *Proceedings of the Fifth International Conference on Operational Research*, Venice, 1969.

A discussion of Beer (1969).

————, and P. Rivett, *A Manager's Guide to Operations Research*, Wiley, New York, 1963.

A brief nontechnical introduction to the subject, written for managers and students of management.

Ansoff, H. I., "A Quasi-Analytic Method for Long-Range Planning," in C. W. Churchman and M. Verhulst (Eds.), *Management Sciences: Models and Techniques*, Vol. 2, Pergamon, New York, 1960, pp. 229–251.

A compromise betwen what is called the "operations research" and "heuristic" approaches to planning. It is process, rather than goal, oriented, uses qualitative judgments as well as quantification, maintains continuous feedback between analysis and problem formulation, tests several objectives simultaneously, divides strategic problems into internal and external, and produces a family of solutions from which one is selected by a weighting procedure. The procedure is methodical without being mathematically rigorous. The similarity of this approach to adaptivizing will be apparent.

————, Corporate Strategy: An Analytical Approach to Business Policy for Growth and Expansion, McGraw-Hill, New York, 1965.

A basic work on strategic planning. It presents no technical obstacles for managers to hurdle. This is an extended treatment of the material presented in the preceding article.

————, and R. C. Brandenburg, "A Program of Research in Business Planning," Management Science, 13 (1967), B219–B239.

I quote from the authors' abstract: ". . . we have constructed a comprehensive program for research on planning. Some parts of the program are being actively pursued, some are still in need of attention. It is our hope that this paper will . . . help give the business planner a sense of unique identity, and that it will provide him with a research program which he can pursue in strengthening this identity." I think they succeed. The article is nontechnical and has a very useful set of references on planning research.

————, and ————, "A Language for Organzational Design," to appear in Proceedings of the OECD Working Symposium on Long-Range Forecasting and Planning (1968), Office of Economic Cooperation and Development, Paris.

A discussion of basic concepts and categories that are useful in the analysis and design of organizational structures.

Beer, Stafford, Decision and Control, Wiley, New York, 1966.

The most comprehensive and penetrating analysis of what operations research and cybernetics are all about, and what they have to offer management. The book is philosophically, rather than technically, oriented and is beautifully written.

————, Management Science: The Business Use of Operations Research, Aldus, London, 1967.

An abbreviated and popularized version of the preceding reference. I suggest trying the longer version first.

————, "The Aborting Corporate Plan," to appear in Proceedings of *the OECD Working Symposium on Long-Range Forecasting and Planning* (1968), Office of Economic Cooperation and Development, Paris.

A fresh and very provocative design of an adaptive organization with a matching concept of planning for it. Computers play a central role in this design.

————, "Planning as a Process of Adaptation," to appear in *Proceedings of the Fifth International Conference on Operational Research*, Venice, 1969.

A shorter version of the preceding with amplification of some points.

Bolan, R. S., "Emerging Views of Planning, *AIP* (American Institute of Planners) *Journal*, July 1967, 233–245.

Although this article deals with city planning, it provides one of the best critical reviews of alternative styles of planning that I have seen. Its applicability to corporate planning is apparent. The article also points to "possible directions for a broader, more detailed conceptual framework for the planning process."

Branch, M. C., *Planning: Aspects and Applications*, Wiley, New York, 1966.

The only attempt of which I am aware to identify and deal with principles applicable to project, city, corporate, and military planning. After an opening discussion of the very general characteristics of planning that are common to its different forms, there follows an analysis of it in each of its forms.

Churchman, C. W., *Prediction and Optimal Decision*, Prentice-Hall, Englewood Cliffs, N.J., 1961.

In my opinion the best available exposition and analysis of the limits of current optimizing methodology. It formulates more questions than it answers, but these questions are more instructive than most people's answers. Managers should be particularly interested in Chapter 3, "Profits and Values," but they should try more than this. Even though nontechnical, it is a hard book to read, but it is more than worth the effort to do so.

————, "The Case against Planning," *Management Decision*, **2** (1968), 74–77.

An exciting challenge directed at five axioms of modern management philosophy. The axioms are turned upside down and defended in this position. A sample: "The so-called goals (profit, pleasure, and learning) are really the means, the means whereby people can contribute to life's plans. It is contribution which is the goal, because contribution is the full expression of each one's individuality. We create problems and attempt to solve them in order to contribute."

————, *Challenge to Reason*, McGraw-Hill, New York, 1968.

More upsetting essays that help us appraise ourselves honestly. The 16 essays are in 3 parts: I—Science and Management, II—the Maximum Loop, and III—The Ethics of Whole Systems.

Cooper, W. W., H. J. Leavitt, and M. W. Shelly, II (Eds.), *New Perspectives in Organizational Research*, Wiley, New York, 1964.

A collection of papers that provides a very good view of the past and present of organizational research. The bibliography contains 617 items.

Cummings, L. L., and W. E. Scott (Eds.), *Readings in Organizational Behavior and Human Performance*, Richard D. Irwin, Homewood, Ill., 1969.

A very well organized set of readings that is bound to contain much of interest and use to almost anyone concerned with organizations.

Dale, Ernest, *Longe-Range Planning*, British Institute of Management, London, 1967.

A brief treatment of planning that contrasts in many ways with the treatment here. The descriptions of what a number of major corporations actually do in planning are particularly useful.

Drucker, P. F., "Long-Range Planning: Challenge to Management Science," *Management Science*, **5** (1959), 238–249.

In his usual thoughtful way Drucker defines "long-range planning," discusses why it is needed, what is needed to do it, and why it is an opportunity for, and challenge to, management science.

Emery, F. E., "The Democratization of the Workplace," *Manpower and Applied Psychology*, **1** (1967), 118–129.

A history of the development of Tavistock Institute's approach to the organization of work. Applications in England, India, Norway, Ireland, and Holland are reviewed. The trials and tribulations of a still evolving concept and theory are discussed with a disarming and instructive frankness.

————, "The Next Thirty Years: Concepts, Methods, and Anticipations," *Human Relations*, **20** (1967), 199–236.

This article is concerned with the concept and methodology of long-range forecasting of large-scale societal changes. However, it it is applicable to organizations that are smaller than society. It is meant for professional planners rather than managers but its profundity merits the effort it might require. The article is not technical, but it is very tightly argued and hence requires study and reflection in addition to reading.

———— (Ed.), *Systems Thinking*, Penguin, Harmondsworth, England, 1969.

All the articles in this set of readings are worthwhile, particularly the next two listed.

————, and E. L. Trist, "The Causal Texture of Organizational Environments," in F. E. Emery (Ed.), *Systems Thinking*, Penguin, Harmondsworth, England, 1969, pp. 241–257.

————, and ————, "Socio-Technical Systems," in F. E. Emery (Ed.), *Systems Thinking*, Penguin, Harmondsworth, England, 1969, pp. 281–296.

These theoretical articles by Emery and Trist provide more insight into the sources and nature of managements' problems than any other articles I know of. They also have important things to say about the kind of managerial orientation toward these problems that can produce effective results. Not easy reading.

Emery, J. C., *Organizational Planning and Control: Theory and Technology*, Ph.D. Thesis, Massachusetts Institute of Technology, Cambridge, September 1965.

A conceptual model of multilevel planning and control and the development of a supporting information system. The role of man-machine planning models is examined. An outline of such a system for financial budgeting is provided.

Ewing, D. W. (Ed.), *Long-Range Planning for Management*, Harper and Row, New York, revised edition, 1958.

A collection of articles that contain enough good ones to make it worthwhile.

Forrester, J. W., "A New Corporate Design," *Industrial Management Review*, **7** (1965), 5–17.

The essential characteristics of this heretical design are (a) decentralized profit centers, (b) the separation of policy making and decision making, (c) freedom of access to information, (d) elimination of internal monopolies, (e) balancing reward and risk,

(f) increased mobility of the individual, and (g) integration of education into corporate life.

Friend, J. K., and W. N. Jessop, *Local Government and Strategic Choice*, Tavistock, London, 1969.

Although this book deals with city planning, it develops a concept of adaptive planning that is widely applicable. The procedures are effectively illustrated by applications to the city of Coventry, England.

Glover, W. S., and R. L. Ackoff, "Five-Year Planning for an Integrated Operation," in *Proceedings of the Conference on Case Studies in Operations Research*, Case Institute of Technology, Cleveland, 1956, pp. 38–47.

A nontechnical account of the preparation of a five-year plan for General Electric's Lamp Division.

Hekiman, J. S., and H. Mentzberg, "The Planning Dilemma," *Management Review*, **57** (1968), 4–17.

A good discussion of why many planners fail to serve the needs of management, and what can be done about it.

Hetrick, J. C., *A Formal Model for Long-Range Planning*, in John Blood, Jr. (Ed.), *Management Science in Planning and Control*, Technical Association of the Pulp and Paper Industry, New York, 1969, pp. 1–38.

A plan for planning that makes use of five different types of mathematical models. They cover (a) definition of corporate objectives and of the nature of the corporation, (b) relationship of the corporation to the economy, (c) consistency of (a) and (b), (d) definition of opportunities, and (e) evaluation of opportunities. The presentation is not technical.

Hirschman, A. D., and C. E. Lindblom, "Economic Development, Research and Development, Policy Making: Some Convergent Views," in F. E. Emery (Ed.), *Systems Thinking*, Penguin, Harmondsworth, England, 1969, pp. 351–371.

A strong argument for satisficing (called "disjointed incrementalism" and "mutual adjustment") sprinkled with a dash of adaptivizing, and against optimizing (called "synoptic decision making"). A longer and later version can be found in Lindblom (1965).

Ireson, W. G., "Preparation for Business in Engineering Schools," in F. C. Pierson et al., *The Education of American Businessmen*, McGraw-Hill, New York, 1959, p. 507 f.

Referred to in Chapter 3. Otherwise not relevant.

Isenson, R. S., "Technological Forecasting in Perspective," *Management Science*, **13** (1966), B70–B83.

Jantsch, Eric, *Technological Forecasting in Perspective*, Office of Economic Cooperation and Development, Paris, 1967.

The Isenson and Jantsch works critically review and constructively evaluate the various techniques of forecasting future technology. They provide a good introduction to the subject and the literature on it.

Kahn, H., and A. T. Wiener, *The Year 2000*, Macmillan, New York, 1967.

So much has been written and said about this one that nothing need be added.

Lindblom, C. E., *The Intelligence of Democracy*, The Free Press, New York, 1965.

See comments on Hirschman and Lindblom (1969).

Myers, M. Scott, "Who Are Your Motivated Workers?" *Harvard Business Review*, **42** (1964), 73–88.

The results of a six-year study at Texas Instruments reveal some forces that motivate workers and some that do not.

———, "Conditions for Manager Motivation," *Harvard Business Review*, **44** (1966), 58–71.

A good application of behavioral science to an important class of workers, managers.

Nadler, Gerald, "An Investigation of Design Methodology," *Management Science*, **13** (1967), B642–B655.

A methodology for designing and engineering projects, but the relevance to organizational design is apparent, particularly the discussion of "ideal system development."

Novick, David, "The Origin and History of Program Budgeting," *California Management Review*, **11** (1968), 7–12.

———, "Long-Range Planning through Program Budgeting," to appear in *Proceedings of the OECD Working Symposium on Long-Range Forecasting and Planning*, (1968), Office of Economic Cooperation and Development, Paris.

These two articles provide a good introduction to this popular technique.

Orden, Alex, *Unified Representation of Managerial Systems,* Report 6843, Department of Economics and Graduate School of Business, University of Chicago, November 1968.

Presents a useful technique for representing graphically and tabularly the several dimensions of managerial activity.

Schlesinger, J. R., *Organizational Structures and Planning,* RAND, P–3316, February 25, 1966.

Consideration of the influence that organizational structure (primarily military) has on planning, and a search for that structure most conducive to successful planning. See in particular his discussion of "Cook's-Tour Planning" and "Lewis-and-Clark Planning." The first is characteristic of satisficers. The second is used more by optimizers and adaptivizers.

Sengupta, S. S., and R. L. Ackoff, "Systems Theory from an OR Point of View," *IEEE Transactions on Systems Science and Cybernetics,* SSC–1 (1965), 9–13.

A brief technical presentation of the theory of organizational structure discussed in Chapter 5.

Steiner, G. A., *Top Management Planning, Macmillan,* New York, 1969.

The most comprehensive treatment of planning of which I am aware. It deals with both concepts and techniques. Particular attention is given to quantitative methods and the use of the behavioral sciences. It concludes with an extensive bibliography of about 700 items.

Trist, E. L., "The Challenge of the Next Thirty Years: A Social Psychological Viewpoint," a talk delivered at the Annual Meeting and Conference of the Town Planning Institute of Canada, June 26–28, 1968.

A penetrating look at the social conditions that are likely to develop over the next few decades. It provides a useful backdrop against which corporate planning can be carried on.

———, G. W. Higgin, H. Murray, and A. B. Pollack, *Organizational Choice,* Tavistock, London, 1963.

A classic sociotechnical study of capabilities of groups at the coal face under changing technologies. Part I provides a good exposition of the sociotechnical approach.

Vickers, Sir Geoffrey, *The Undirected Society*, Basic Books, New York, 1959.

———, *The Art of Judgment*, Basic Books, New York, 1965.

———, *Toward a Sociology of Management*, Basic Books, New York, 1967.

———, *Value Systems and Social Process*, Basic Books, New York, 1968.

Vickers is one of the most profound contemporary philosophers of management (public and private). He has very deep insight into what is happening to our society and the organizations in it. He makes liberal use of important new ideas produced by contemporary technology and the behavioral sciences.

Vogel, E. H., "Creative Marketing and Management Science," *Management Decision*, 3 (1969), 21–25.

A creative manager's look at his use of the management sciences in marketing a consumer product. His observations on how to use these sciences effectively are applicable to any function and any kind of business, public or private.

Waid, C., D. F. Clark, and R. L. Ackoff, "Allocation of Sales Effort in the Lamp Division of the General Electric Company," *Operations Research*, 4 (1956), 629–647.

A study referred to in Chapter 4.

Weinberg, R. S., "Multiple Factor Break-Even Analysis: The Application of OR Techniques to Basic Problems of Management Planning and Control," *Operations Research*, 4 (1956), 152–186.

———, "The Uses and Limitations of Mathematical Models for Market Planning," in *An Analytical Approach to Advertising Expenditures*, Association of National Advertisers, New York, 1960, pp. 3–34.

———, "Management Science and Marketing Strategy," in Wroe Alderson and S. J. Shapiro (Eds.), *Marketing and the Computer*, Prentice-Hall, Englewood Cliffs, N.J., 1963, pp. 98–127.

The author of these three articles is a management scientist who is now a corporate vice president in charge of planning. His articles reflect the two-sidedness of his experience. They are both systematic and pragmatic.

Wiles, P. J. D., "Economic Activation, Planning, and the Social Order," in B. M. Gross (Ed.), *Action under Planning*, McGraw-Hill, New York, 1967, pp. 138–185.

Referred to in Chapter 3.

AUTHOR INDEX

Ackoff, R. L., 32, 48, 59, 74, 146, 151, 153
Alderson, W., 154
Ansoff, H. I., 64, 146, 147

Beer, S., 126, 146, 147, 148
Bierce, A., 12
Blood, J., Jr., 151
Bolan, R. S., 148
Branch, M. C., 146, 148
Brandenburg, R. C., 147

Churchman, C. W., 146, 148, 149
Clark, D. F., 48, 154
Cooper, W. W., 87, 149
Crozier, M., 15–16
Cummings, L. L., 108, 149

Daedalus, 57
Dale, E., 149
Drucker, P. F., 149

Emery, F. E., 18, 81, 101, 108, 149–150
Emery, J. C., 150
Ewing, D. W., 150

Forrester, J. W., 150–151
Friend, J. K., 151

Glover, W. S., 48, 74, 151
Gross, B. M., 154

Hekiman, J. S., 151
Hetrick, J. C., 64, 151
Higgin, G. W., 153

Hirschman, A. D., 151

Ireson, W. G., 61, 151
Isenson, R. S., 152

Jantsch, E., 57, 152
Jessop, W. N., 151

Kahn, H., 57, 152

Leavitt, H. J., 87, 149
Lindblom, C. E., 151, 152

Mentzberg, H., 151
Murray, H., 153
Myers, M., 108, 152

Nadler, Gerald, 63, 152
Novick, David, 152

The Observer, 84
Orden, Alex, 152

Pollack, A. B., 153

Rivett, P., 146

Schlesinger, J. R., 153
Scott, W. E., 108, 149
Sengupta, S. S., 153
Shapiro, S. J., 154
Shelly, M. W., II, 87, 149
Steiner, G. A., 146, 153
Sun Tzu, 138

Trist, E. L., 15–16, 81, 150, 153

Verhulst, M., 146
Vickers, Sir Geoffrey, 24, 153–154
Vogel, E. H., 48, 51, 154

Waid, C., 48, 154
Weinberg, R. S., 154
Wiener, A. T., 57, 152
Wiles, P. J. D., 55, 154

SUBJECT INDEX

Despite an abundance of literature on the subject of corporate planning, it is common to find confusion among managers concerning what a plan should contain, how planning should be conducted, and what values can be derived from it. Avoiding both extremes of easy platitudes and technicalities, which account for so much of the planning literature, an outstanding authority in the field explains in simple, straightforward language what should be done, who should do it, and why.

Unlike many other books in the field this book is not merely a description of current practices. It develops a new concept of planning—Adaptive Planning—in a systematic way and attempts to exploit the management and behavioral sciences to the fullest. Throughout, illustrations are used extensively to point up the logic of various processes.

A Concept of Corporate Planning distinguishes between tactical and strategic planning. The following parts of the planning process are discussed in detail.

- —how to specify objectives and goals
- —how to specify the means by which objectives and goals are to be obtained
- —how to specify resource requirements; how they are obtained and allocated
- —how to design the management system and organizational structure required to carry out the plan
- —how to maintain and control the plan under changing conditions

The result of many years experience in all aspects of corporate planning, this systematic and practical volume will be a challenging and valuable addition to every manager's working library.